Building job sites with Joomla!

Establish and be in charge of a job site using easily adaptable Joomla! extensions.

Santonu Kumar Dhar

BIRMINGHAM - MUMBAI

Building job sites with Joomla!

First published: September 2010

Production Reference: 1160910

Published by Packt Publishing Ltd.
32 Lincoln Road
Olton
Birmingham, B27 6PA, UK.

ISBN 978-1-849512-22-0

www.packtpub.com

Cover Image by John M. Quick (john.m.quick@gmail.com)

Credits

Author
Santonu Kumar Dhar

Reviewer
Nakul Ganesh S

Acquisition Editor
Dilip Venkatesh

Development Editor
Meeta Rajani

Technical Editors
Ajay Shanker
Pooja Pande

Copy Editor
Lakshmi Menon

Indexer
Monica Ajmera Mehta

Editorial Team Leader
Akshara Aware

Project Team Leader
Priya Mukherji

Project Coordinator
Vincila Colaco

Proofreader
Cecere Mario

Graphics
Nilesh Mohite

Production Coordinator
Melwyn D'sa

Cover Work
Melwyn D'sa

About the Author

Santonu Kumar Dhar was born on 16 June 1987, in Comilla, Bangladesh. He developed an interest for websites in 1995 when he saw a television program on website technology. He got an opportunity to explore the computer world ten years later in 2005. He started web designing in 2006 and he has operated several websites since 2007. Now his web development skills include PHP/MYSQL, XHTML, CSS, JavaScript, WML, Joomla!, and other CMS such as Drupal and Wordpress. Besides this he also has a good fundamental knowledge of programming with Java, C/C++, and VB.Net. He is interested more in the development of web applications than desktop applications.

He is also co-founder Chairman and Editor In Chief of the fashion magazine "HAULE HAULE" (ISSN: 2078-8797), Haule Haule Magazine, Entertainment, and Media Relations, Inc. 848 N. Rainbow Blvd. Suite #1711, Las Vegas, NV 89107, USA, http://www.haulehaule.com.

Acknowledgement

My love and thanks to my parents, relatives and friends. "Thank you! For supporting me".

I would specially like to thank my uncle Hari Narayan Das, Kallol Majumder, my cousins Dr. Rajib Das Dip, Mithila Das, Sourav Das, and my brother-in-law Amit Kumar Raut for inspiring me a lot.

Thanks to Rajesh Bhowmik; he is not only my relative but also a good friend and supported me all the time.

I would like to thank the Packt team, especially Priya Mukherji, Dilip Venkatesh, and Vincila Colaco for their guidance and co-operation.

Special thanks to Ulas Ulkane and his team at InstantPHP, for providing necessary information and technical support.

I also appreciate the readers of this book and I hope it will be helpful to them.

Finally, thanks to all the reviewers of this book for their comments, suggestions, and recommendations.

About the Reviewer

Nakul Ganesh is a 22 year old programmer from Mysore, India. He has a Bachelor's Degree in Information Science Engineering from The Visvesvaraya Technological University (India). He is an avid open source contributor and has twice been a Student Contract worker for Joomla! under the Google Summer of Code Program. Nakul is an ardent fan of PHP and Python and is currently working on a Multi-Touch Python library. You can reach him at nakulgan@gmail.com.

Table of Contents

Preface

Welcome to the first edition of *Building Jobsites with Joomla! 1.5*. This books provides a new approach for developing jobsites with Joomla!, a popular CMS program that became an affordable solution for website development. Joomla! is absolutely free and available with a GNU/GPL license. It not only saves money and time, but also saves a lot of effort that goes into development. In order for a Joomla! website to function as a jobsite, we need a third-party extension. In this book, we have covered the uses of Instant Php's jobsite extension Jobs! Pro 1.3.2 along with Joomla 1.5. Jobs! is one of the most popular and user-friendly extension's that provides all the features and functionalities of a jobsite. This book will provide stepwise tutorial on administrating Joomla! and Jobs! Pro control panel for building and developing your jobsite properly.

Whether you are reading this book on your own or using it as a companion to Joomla! learning course, I hope it gives you a good head start and that you have fun in the process.

What this book covers

Chapter 1, Installing and Configuring Joomla! 1.5 and Jobs! Pro, covers the basics of Joomla! 1.5 installation. You will also learn to use Jobs! Pro extension along with Joomla!. This chapter briefly describes the method of managing sections, categories, and content. It also describes how to manage extensions and add modules.

Chapter 2, Control Panel Interface, introduces you to Joomla! 1.5 administrator panel and Jobs! Pro control panel interface. After finishing this chapter, you can administrate and drive out your Joomla! jobsite easily.

Chapter 3, Designing a Jobsite Template, explains the basics of creating a Joomla! 1.5 template. After finishing this chapter, the basics of the template design in Joomla! 1.5 will be clear.

Chapter 4, Changing Configuration Settings, provides a step-by-step guideline to configuring your Joomla! jobsite with Global Configuration and Jobs! Pro configuration settings.

Chapter 5, Managing Jobs, Job Types, and Categories, is written for a practical approach. After completing this chapter you will learn managing jobs, job types, and categories from Jobs! Pro control panel.

Chapter 6, Managing Countries and Companies, covers adding a new country and managing list countries from the administrator panel. You will also learn how to manage company countries.

Chapter 7, Managing Email and Application Status, provides guidelines to create an e-mail template that will be used to respond to the applicants. You will also learn how to manage applications and its status. After reading this chapter, you will easily be able to manage your e-mail templates, applications, and application status.

Chapter 8, User Registration, Credits, Resume fields, and Education Levels, explains some complex and critical tasks, such as user registration system, managing employer credits, managing resume fields, and education levels. After completing this chapter, you will learn registering an employer or a jobseeker and managing the credit system. You will also learn to add or remove resume fields, resume field category, and education levels.

Chapter 9, Managing Cover Letter, Resume, and Resume Files, talks about viewing, adding, deleting, publishing and unpublishing cover letters, resumes, and resume files. After finishing this chapter, you can manage cover letters, resumes, and resume files.

Chapter 10, Search Engine Optimization (SEO), covers SEO, making SEO strategy, how to choose the right keywords, inserting the title and metadata in your Joomla! jobsite, changing basic SEO settings, making SEF URLs, creating an XML or an HTML site map, and submitting site maps and websites to search engines.

Appendix A, Online Resources, provides some website listings for further reading.

Appendix B, Search Engine Stop Words, provides a list of search engine stop words, which will help you to avoid using these words as keywords in SEO.

What you need for this book

You can use any platform such as Windows, Linux, MAC, or any other operating system. You will need the following:

- Joomla! 1.5.20 or higher: Joomla! is a popular CMS program. You can download the latest version of Joomla! freely from its official download page, `http://www.joomla.org/download.html`.

- Jobs! Pro 1.3.2 or higher: Jobs! is a popular Joomla! extension for building a jobsite. You can get it from developer Instant Php's website, `http://www.instantphp.com`. It is available only with a commercial license.

- XAMPP 1.7.x or higher: XAMPP is a popular server solution. It comes equipped with Apache HTTP Server, PHP, and MySQL. You can download the latest version of XAMPP 1.7.x from the Apache Friends website, `http://www.apachefriends.org/en/xampp.html`.

- FileZilla FTP: FileZilla is a free FTP program available for different operating systems, including Windows, Linux, and Mac OS. You can get it from `http://filezilla-project.org/`.

Who this book is for

If you are looking to build and manage a jobsite using Joomla! extensions, then this book is for you. Prior knowledge of using extensions is not expected, but Joomla! basics will be required.

Conventions

In this book, you will find a number of styles of text that distinguish between different kinds of information. Here are some examples of these styles, and an explanation of their meaning.

Code words in text are shown as follows: "Add a `<param>` element for each parameter that you want to define and insert these between `<params>...</params>` tags."

A block of code is set as follows:

```
<?xml version="1.0" encoding="utf-8"?>
<!DOCTYPE install PUBLIC "-//Joomla! 1.5//DTD template 1.0//EN"
"http://www.joomla.org/xml/dtd/1.5/template-install.dtd">
```

Any command-line input or output is written as follows:

```
tar xvfz xampp-linux-1.7.3a.tar.gz -C /opt
```

New terms and **important words** are shown in bold. Words that you see on the screen, in menus or dialog boxes for example, appear in the text like this: "Now click on **Save** to save everything."

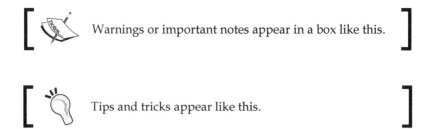

Warnings or important notes appear in a box like this.

Tips and tricks appear like this.

Reader feedback

Feedback from our readers is always welcome. Let us know what you think about this book—what you liked or may have disliked. Reader feedback is important for us to develop titles that you really get the most out of.

To send us general feedback, simply send an e-mail to feedback@packtpub.com, and mention the book title via the subject of your message.

If there is a book that you need and would like to see us publish, please send us a note in the **SUGGEST A TITLE** form on www.packtpub.com or e-mail suggest@packtpub.com.

If there is a topic that you have expertise in and you are interested in either writing or contributing to a book on, see our author guide on www.packtpub.com/authors.

Customer support

Now that you are the proud owner of a Packt book, we have a number of things to help you to get the most from your purchase.

Downloading the example code for this book

You can download the example code files for all Packt books you have purchased from your account at http://www.packtpub.com. If you purchased this book elsewhere, you can visit http://www.packtpub.com/support and register to have the files e-mailed directly to you.

Errata

Although we have taken every care to ensure the accuracy of our content, mistakes do happen. If you find a mistake in one of our books—maybe a mistake in the text or the code—we would be grateful if you would report this to us. By doing so, you can save other readers from frustration and help us improve subsequent versions of this book. If you find any errata, please report them by visiting http://www.packtpub.com/support, selecting your book, clicking on the **errata submission** link, and entering the details of your errata. Once your errata are verified, your submission will be accepted and the errata will be uploaded on our website, or added to any list of the existing errata, under the Errata section of that title. Any existing errata can be viewed by selecting your title from http://www.packtpub.com/support.

Piracy

Piracy of copyright material on the Internet is an ongoing problem across all media. At Packt, we take the protection of our copyright and licenses very seriously. If you come across any illegal copies of our works, in any form, on the Internet, please provide us with the location address or website name immediately so that we can pursue a remedy.

Please contact us at copyright@packtpub.com with a link to the suspected pirated material.

We appreciate your help in protecting our authors and our ability to bring you valuable content.

Questions

You can contact us at questions@packtpub.com if you are having a problem with any aspect of the book, and we will do our best to address it.

1
Installing and Configuring Joomla! 1.5 and Jobs! Pro 1.3.2

Joomla! has earned a reputation of being one of the most powerful CMS programs around, as its core team emerged from another popular open source **Content Management System (CMS)** program called Mambo. Joomla! was downloaded more than 2.5 million times within the first year of its release. It has over 200,000 community users and contributors. Although Joomla! is so popular, building jobsites with Joomla! is a new concept.

To build a jobsite, you need to use a jobs and recruitment extension (such as Jobs!, Jobline!, or JS Jobs) in your Joomla! website. We will use the Jobs! extension because it provides all of the functionalities that a professional jobsite should have. It provides graphical user interface for administrator, employer, and jobseeker. Before we start how to develop a jobsite with Joomla!, we need to install and configure Joomla! 1.5 and Jobs! extension along with all of its modules.

This chapter explains:

- Prerequisites for installation of Joomla! 1.5 and Jobs!
- Setting up a local server environment
- Uploading installation packages and files to server
- Creating database and user for the database
- Installing and configuring Joomla! 1.5
- Managing sections, categories, and articles
- Managing extensions
- Installing and configuring Jobs!
- Adding modules

Introduction

You may have various approaches for building a jobsite, with job search and registration facilities for users and providing several services to your clients such as job posting, online application process, resume search, and so on. Joomla! is one of the best approaches and an affordable solution for building your jobsite, even if you are a novice to Joomla!. This is because Joomla! is a free, open source Content Management System (CMS), which provides one of the most powerful web application development frameworks available today. These are all reasons for building a jobsite with Joomla!:

- It has a friendly interface for all types of users—designers, developers, authors, and administrators.

- This CMS is growing rapidly and improving since its release. Joomla! is designed to be easy to install and set up even if you're not an advanced user.

- Another advantage is that you need less time and effort to build a jobsite with Joomla!.

You need to use a Joomla! jobsite extension to build your jobsite and you can use the commercial extension Jobs! because it's fully equipped to operate a jobsite, featuring tools to manage jobs, resumes, applications, and subscriptions. If you are looking for a jobsite such as Monster, Career Builder, a niche jobs listing such as Tech Crunch, or just posting job ads on your company site, Jobs! is an ideal solution. To know more about this extension, visit its official website http://www.instantphp.com/.

Jobs! has two variations—**Jobs! Pro** and **Jobs! Basic**. The Jobs! Pro provides some additional features and facilities, which are not available in Jobs! Basic. You can use any one of them, depending upon your needs and budget. But if you need full control over your jobsite and more customization facilities, then Jobs! Pro is recommended. You can install Jobs! component and its modules easily, like any other Joomla! extension. You need to spend only a few minutes to install and configure Joomla! 1.5 and Jobs! Pro 1.3 or Jobs! Basic 1.0. It is a stepwise setup process. But first you must ensure that your system meets all the requirements that are recommended by developers.

Prerequisites for installation of Joomla! 1.5 and Jobs!

Joomla! is written in PHP and mainly uses MySQL database to store and manipulate information. Before installing Joomla! 1.5 and Jobs! extension, we need a server environment, that includes the following:

Software/Application	Minimum Requirement	Recommended Version	Website
PHP	5	5.2	`http//php.net`
MySQL	4.1 or above	5	`http://dev.mysql.com/downloads/mysql/5.0.html`
Apache	1.3 or above		`http://httpd.apache.org`
IIS	6	7	`http://www.iis.net/`
mod_mysql			
mod_xml			
mod_zlib			

You must ensure that you have the MySQL, XML, and zlib functionality enabled within your PHP installation. This is controlled within the `php.ini` file.

Setting up a local server environment

In order to run Joomla! properly, we need a server environment with pre-installed PHP and MySQL. In this case, you can use a virtual server or can choose other hosting options. But if you want to try out Joomla! on your own computer before using a remote server, we can set up a local server environment.

To set up a server environment, we can use **XAMPP** solution. It comes equipped with Apache HTTP server, PHP, and MySQL. Installing these components individually is quite difficult and needs more time and effort.

To install XAMPP, download the latest version of XAMPP 1.7.x from the Apache friends website: `http://www.apachefriends.org/en/xampp.html`.

Windows operating system users can install XAMPP for Windows in two different variations—self-extracting RAR archive and ZIP archive.

If you want to use self-extracting RAR archive, first download the `.exe` file and then follow these steps:

1. Run the installer file, choose a directory, and click on the **Install** button.

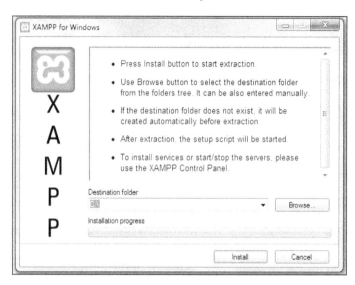

After extracting XAMPP, the setup script `setup_xampp.bat` will start automatically.

2. After the installation is done, click on **Start | All Programs | Apache Friends | XAMPP | XAMPP Control Pane**.

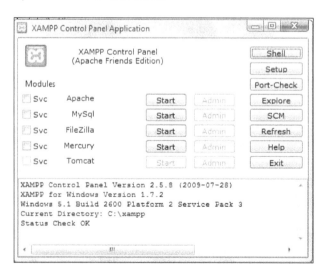

3. Start Apache and MySQL by clicking on the **Start** buttons beside each item. If prompted by Windows Firewall, click on the **Unblock** button.

   For more information on installing XAMPP on Windows or troubleshooting, go to the Windows FAQs page: `http://www.apachefriends.org/en/faq-xampp-windows.html`.

   If you are using Linux platform, download the compressed `.tar.gz` file and follow these steps for installation:

4. Go to a Linux shell and log in as the system administrator root:

   ```
   su
   ```

5. Extract the downloaded archive file to `/opt`:

   ```
   tar xvfz xampp-linux-1.7.3a.tar.gz -C /opt
   ```

   XAMPP is now installed in the `/opt/lampp` directory.

6. To start XAMPP, call the command:

   ```
   /opt/lampp/lampp start
   ```

   You should now see something similar to the following on your screen:

   ```
   Starting XAMPP 1.7.3a...
   LAMPP: Starting Apache...
   LAMPP: Starting MySQL...
   LAMPP started.
   ```

For more information on installing XAMPP on Linux or troubleshooting, go to the Linux FAQs page: `http://www.apachefriends.org/en/faq-xampp-linux.html`.

If you want to use XAMPP in MAC operating system, download the `.dmg` file and follow these steps:

1. Open the DMG-Image.
2. Drag and drop the XAMPP folder into your `Applications` folder.
3. XAMPP is now installed in the `/Applications/XAMPP` directory.
4. To start XAMPP open XAMPP Control and start Apache and MySQL.
5. After installation of XAMPP in a system, to test your installation, type the following URL in the browser: `http://localhost/`.

You will see the XAMPP start page.

Uploading installation packages and files to server

Now, we need to copy or transfer Joomla! installation package files to server. Before copying the installation package, we must download `Joomla_1.5.15-Stable-Full_Package.zip` from the webpage `http://www.joomla.org/download.html`, and then extract and unzip it. You can use WinZip or WinRAR to unzip these files. After unzipping the files, you have to copy files on your server root folder (for Apache, it is `htdocs` folder). If you are not using the XAMPP or local server environment, you need the **File Transfer Protocol (FTP)** software to transfer files to your server root folder, such as `htdocs` or `wwwroot`. The popular FTP software is FileZilla, which is absolutely free and available for different platforms, including Windows, Linux, and Mac OS. You can get it from the website `http://filezilla-project.org/`.

Creating database and user

Before installing and configuring Joomla! and Jobs! extension, we also need to create a database and a database user. You can easily add a new database and any user by using phpMyAdmin in XAMPP server environment. To add a database, by using **phpMyAdmin**, you must follow the following steps:

- Type the address `http://localhost/phpmyadmin` in the web browser. The front page of phpMyAdmin will be displayed.

- Type a name for the database you want to create. For example, **my_db** in the **Create new Database** field and then click on the **Create** button to create the database.

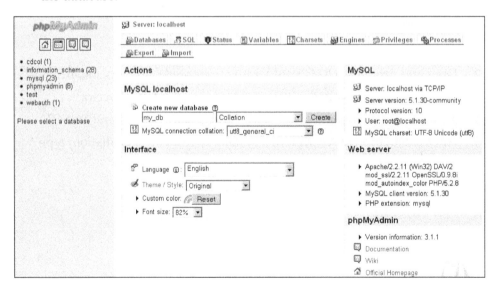

- To be connected with the database, we need a user account. You can add a user account by clicking on the **Privileges** tab of phpMyAdmin.

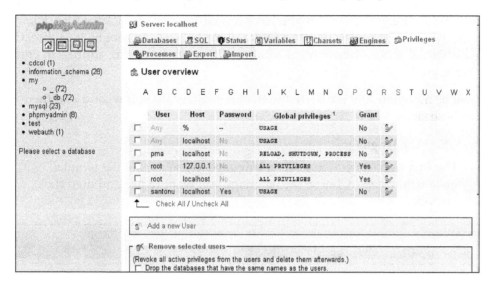

- You will see all users' information. Click on **Add a new User** link of **Privileges** window. After clicking on the link, a new window will appear. Provide the required information in the **Login Information** section of this window and then click on the **Go** button.

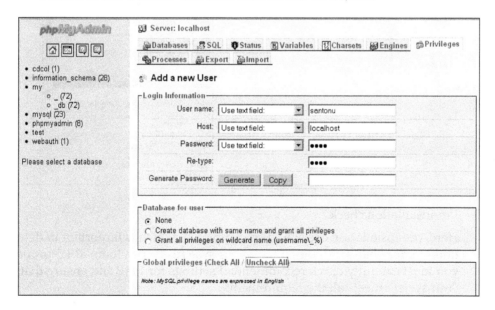

We have now completed the preparation stage of installing Joomla!.

Installing and configuring Joomla! 1.5

We are now ready to install Joomla! 1.5. Open a web browser and type the address of your server directory in which you have copied Joomla!1.5 package files. For example, if you have copied files to a folder named `joomla` in root `htdocs` directory of XAMPP local server environment, you must type the following address in your web browser: `http://localhost/joomla`.

You will be automatically redirected to the Joomla! installation wizard and then follow these steps:

1. Choosing language:

   The first step lets you to select a language to use during the Joomla! installation steps. Choose the language you want to use and then click on **Next**.

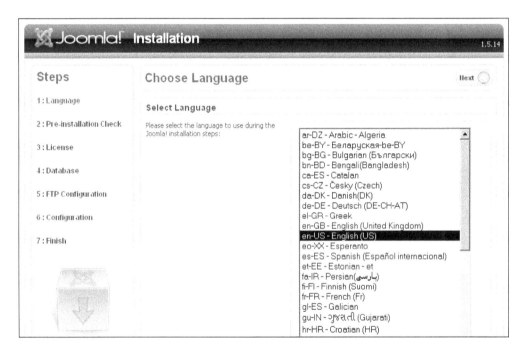

2. Pre-installation check:

   Here, pre-installation check will be completed, which is important to determine compatibility of Joomla! with your system. To run Joomla! 1.5 properly, you must carefully check recommended settings for PHP and ensure that your system meets all the requirements.

If some settings are not the same as recommended, these settings will be highlighted in red. You can solve them by changing the PHP settings in `php.ini` file in your server. You will find the list of the `php.ini` directives that you can set to configure your PHP setup in the following webpage: `http://www.php.net/manual/en/ini.list.php`.

On Unix-based systems (Linux, Mac OS X), attention should be given to writing rights. This is particularly important for the `configuration.php` file. At the end of the installation, this file gets created with its individual values. If the installer does not have writing rights, Joomla! cannot create this file and the installation will fail. If this happens, try to configure the rights appropriately and click on **Check Again**. After checking successfully, click on **Next**.

3. License:

   In this step, you need to carefully read the license agreement and accept it. Joomla! is available with the GNU/GPL license. The **GNU General Public License** (**GNU GPL** or simply **GPL**) is a widely used free software license, originally written for the GNU. For more details, visit the webpage: `http://www.gnu.org/licenses/gpl.html`.

Something similar to the following screenshot will appear. After reading and accepting the license agreement, click on **Next**.

4. Database Configuration:

    In this step, you have to set up Joomla! to connect with database and run on your server. Type the URL of your database host in the **Host Name** field, then provide the username you have created earlier in the **User Name** field; provide also the password in the **Password** field and your database name in the **Database Name** field.

    For example, type something like the following:

    Host Name: `http://localhost`

    Username: Santonu

    Password: 1234

    Database Name: my_db

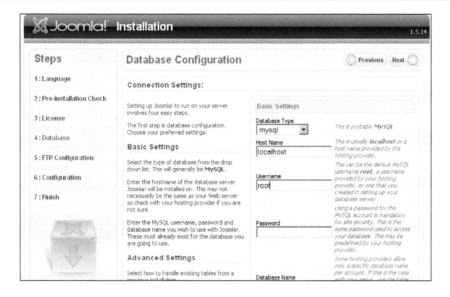

After providing the database information, click on **Next**.

5. FTP Configuration:

To solve the problem of PHP safe-mode restrictions, you can use an FTP layer to upload files and handle all the file system operations. To use an FTP layer, type an FTP username in the **FTP User** field and a password in the **FTP Password** field.

It is always recommended to skip this step. You can enable this anytime from the **Global configuration** window, in case of any security problems. Now click on the **Next** button to go to the next step.

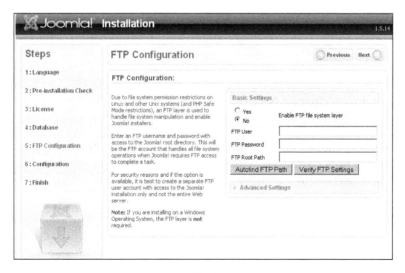

6. Main Configuration:

    This step enables you to configure Joomla! and this is the main configuration step of the Joomla! installation. First, you have to provide the name of your website in the **Site Name** field. This name will normally appear in the title section of a web browser.

    Then provide your e-mail address and also provide admin password and then retype the password in the **Confirm Admin Password** field. By default, your super administrator username is **admin**. You cannot define another username during installation but you can change it later from the admin panel.

    If you are a beginner, you can click on **Install Sample Data** to load sample data and then click on **Next**.

7. Finish:

    In this step, your Joomla! installation steps will be completed **Congratulations! Joomla! is now installed**, as shown in the following screenshot. This means you have successfully completed the installation steps.

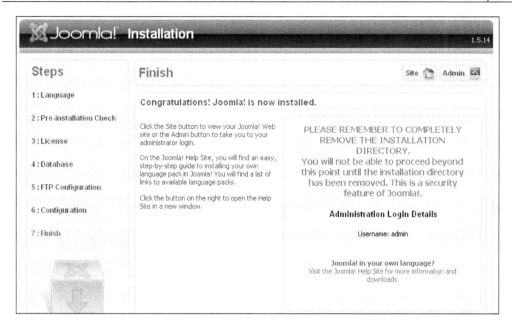

Now you have to remove the Joomla! installation folder first, and then click on the **Site** button to view your Joomla! website or click on the **Admin** button to take a tour of the Joomla! administrator panel. You can easily remove this folder. Go to your server root directory where Joomla! is installed. Delete the entire installation folder.

If you are using a hosting solution instead of a local server, you can remove this folder in two ways:

- By using the **File Manager** tool in your hosting control panel (such as C-Panel, Plesk)
- By using an FTP client (such as FileZilla and SmartFTP)

See *Appendix, Online Resources*, for more information on how to delete files and folders in C-Panel, Plesk, and other control panels. You will also find online resources on how to delete files and folders using an FTP program.

Managing sections, categories, and articles

Joomla! is a popular content management system, so it is mainly used for managing content. You can manage content from the Joomla! backend administrator panel. To go to this area, type in your web browser, the address of the server directory where the `administrator` folder is located. For example, if you have installed Joomla! in the `joomla` directory of local server, then the address is: `http://localhost/ joomla/administrator`.

You will see the **Joomla! Administration Login** screen in your browser window.

Log into the administrator panel as **Super Administrator**. By default, the username is **admin**. Then provide the password that you have created while you were configuring. Before adding an article as content, you must create a section and category for it. You can organize your content by using sections and categories because Joomla! uses a three-tier organization level for articles—**Section | Category | Article**. Any section contains one or more categories, and each category may have articles assigned to it. One article can only be in one category and section.

You can easily add new sections, edit existing sections, publish or unpublish any section, and copy or delete sections from the **Section Manager** window. To manage sections, click on **Contents | Section Manager** (as shown in the following screenshot):

The process of managing categories is quite similar to managing sections. You just need to click on **Contents | Category Manager** to go to **Category Manager** window and then manage your categories.

After creating section and category, to add a new article from admin panel, click on **Contents | Article Manager** (as shown in the following screenshot):

To add a new article, click on the New button in the **Article Manager** window and write your article with a title in **Article: [New]** window WYSISWYG editor area. You must also define the section and category for this article—which you have created earlier—and save this content.

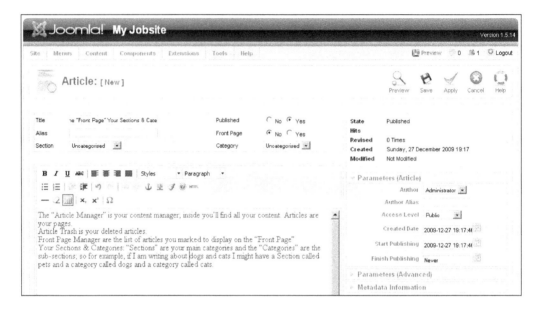

If you want to edit an article, select the article, click on Edit, and then make any changes in the article in **Article: [Edit]** window. **Article Manager** enables you to publish or unpublish an article. You can send an article to trash, copy an article, move an article, and so on. Just select an article and then click on the corresponding buttons.

Managing extensions

Components, modules, plugins, templates, and languages are collectively known as **extensions**. Each of these extensions is used for specific functions:

- Components: It is the largest and the most complex of the extension types. When a Joomla! web page is being loaded, a component is called to render the main page body. For example, the component `com_banners` displays a banner in a web page. Components are divided into two parts—for the administrator and for the frontend website.

- Modules: It is used for page rendering and doesn't need to be linked to anything. It can contain only static HTML, image, or text. For example, `mod_mainmenu` and `mod_banners`.

- Plugins: These were previously known as mambots. Using a plugin allows a developer to change the way their code behaves depending upon which plugins are installed to react to an event.

- Templates: It is basically the design of your Joomla! website. With a template, you can change the look and the feel of your website. Templates have certain fields in which components and modules are shown. You can easily create and customize any template file.

- Languages: Languages can be packaged in two ways—either as a core package or as an extension package—and allow both the Joomla! core as well as third-party components and modules to be localized or internationalized.

To know more about extensions, go to the Joomla! documentation page: `http://docs.joomla.org/Joomla!_Extensions_Defined`.

You can easily manage extensions by using the **Extensions** menu. For example, to install or uninstall any extension, click on the menu **Extension | Install/Uninstall**; to manage modules, click on the **Module Manager**; to manage plugins, click on the **Plugin Manager**; to manage templates, click on the **Template Manager**; and to manage language, click on the **Language Manager**.

Installing and configuring Jobs!

Installation of Jobs! is very simple; you will only need to install using the installer tool of the extensions manager. Before installing and configuring the Jobs! extension, get it from developer InstantPHP's website: `http://www.instantphp.com`. It is available only with a commercial license. Jobs! comes with some modules and plugins. To install and configure Jobs! extension, you need to follow these steps:

1. First click on the menu **Extensions | Install/Uninstall** to open the **Extensions Manager** window, as shown in the following screenshot:

2. In the **Extensions Manager** window, click on **Browse** in the install section and look for the installer file called `com_jobs_XXX.zip` of the Jobs! extension package you have purchased. Then click on **Upload & Install**, as shown in the following screenshot:

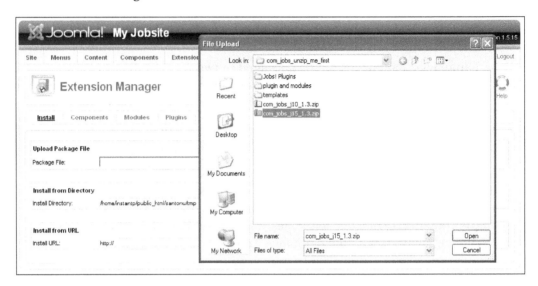

 If you get an error during installation stating that the folder `com_jobs` is already in use, you must check that `.../components/com_jobs` folder must not be used by any other component.

When the installation completes successfully, you will see the message **Install Component Success**. Now, you need to install some modules. Modules and plugins are also extensions, so you can install all modules and plugins in the same way. Jobs! comes with some modules, plugins, and templates. You will find them in a folder named `Plugin and Modules` in the Jobs! extension package. You need to install some important modules to make your website functional. The Jobs! module—`mod_jobs`—is one of them and it is the main module. You must install it to access the Jobs! component in the website's frontend. In this way, you can install other modules such as search module, categories module, latest jobs, random jobs, and so on. Also, you can install any plugin and template file later. If you need more information and support you can go to InstantPHP's support page: `http://www.instantphp.com/support/21-jobs-support.html`.

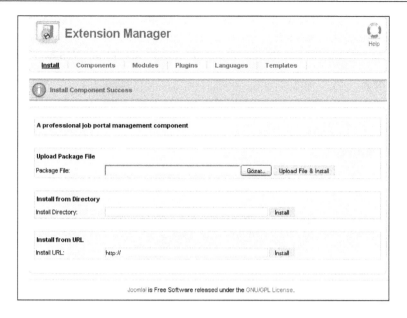

3. Jobs! is now installed along with some of its modules. After installing the Jobs! Component, you need to configure it. First, add at least one application status and be sure that it's published because it is one of the key features of Jobs! and so it is essential to enable the jobseeker application system. It will set the default status when an application is received from a jobseeker. To add a new application status, click on the menu **Components | Jobs | List Application Status**, as shown in the following screenshot:

After that, click on **Add New** and provide some status name for online application in the new window and save it as published. Application status is a classification of applications received from the candidates. Some basic examples are:

- Pending
- Under review
- Rejected
- Accepted

Click on menu **Components | Jobs | Configuration** and check the **Default Status** drop-down list in the **General Settings** tab of the **Configuration Settings** window. Now select the status name you want to make default and save this setting.

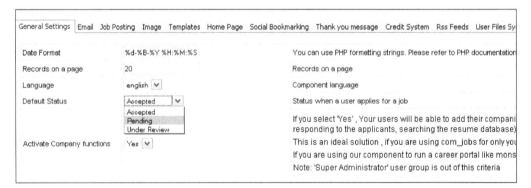

Adding modules

You can easily add and enable modules to the Joomla! website; modules must be installed before enabling them if your installed modules are jobs, search module, and categories module. Enable these modules from the **Module Manager** window. To do this, click on the menu **Extensions | Module Manager**. After that, checkmark the modules you want to enable and click on **Enable**.

Summary

In this chapter, we have learned the basics of Joomla! 1.5 installation. We have also learned how to use Jobs! extension along with Joomla! 1.5. This chapter briefly described the method of managing sections, categories, and content. It also described how to manage extensions and add modules. So if you are a beginner, this information will be helpful to you.

2
Control Panel Interface

Joomla! is a popular CMS, and control panel is an essential part of any CMS. The Joomla! control panel is known as Joomla! administrator panel. We have also installed Jobs! component to build our jobsite. This component provides control panel interface as well. In order to manage your Joomla! jobsite properly, you must familiarize yourselves with the Joomla! 1.5 administrator control panel and Jobs! control panel interface. Joomla! consists of a frontend and a backend. The **frontend** is the website that is easily accessible to visitors or users. The **backend** contains the administration layer of the website, which may not be fully accessible to all users, except the super-administrator. The super-administrator can manage the whole website from this backend control panel.

This chapter gives a brief overview of:

- Joomla! administrator panel, including its menus, submenus, tools, lists, and dialogs
- Jobs! control panel interface, including its buttons, tabs, and tools

Introducing Joomla! administrator panel

To access the administrator login page, you need to type the path of `administrator` directory in the address field. For example, `http://localhost/administrator`. If you are not using the local server, type your web server address instead of `localhost`.

After logging into the Joomla! administrator panel, you will see an interface similar to the next screenshot:

At the top of the screen, you will see a menu bar with menus and submenus. You will also see the following four elements on the right-hand side:

- **Preview** link: It is a link to preview the website's front page.

- Received message counter: It shows how many messages you have received. If no messages are received, it shows a zero (0).

- Users counter: It displays how many users are logged into your site at the moment.

- **Logout** link: This link is used to log out from the administrator panel.

Below the menu bar, you will see buttons such as **Add New Article**, **Article Manager**, **Front Page Manager**, **Section Manager**, **Category Manager**, **Media Manager**, and others. You will also see some drop-down boxes on the right panel, such as **Logged in Users**, **Popular**, **Recent added Articles**, and **Menu Stats**. These drop-down boxes display corresponding status reports.

Menus

Menus are at the top of the menu bar, as shown in the following screenshot. The menu bar contains seven menus — **Site**, **Menus**, **Content**, **Components**, **Extensions**, **Tools**, and **Help**. These menus are named according to their relevance. Following are some examples:

- **Site** menu provides links to manage website users, images or other media files, changing configuration settings, and so on

- **Menus** menu provides links to managing website front page menus with menu items, restoring deleted menus, main menu, and other navigation menus

- **Content** menu provides links to managing articles or contents, and managing sections and categories

- **Components** menu provides the facility to manage website banners, contact details, news feeds, polls, search, and web links

- **Extensions** menu provides links to install or uninstall extensions, manage modules, plugins, templates, and website languages

- **Tools** menu provides links to some additional features such as messages, cache files, and others

- **Help** menu provides links to helpful information and online help resource link

Submenus

Submenus are part of a menu; they provide links to corresponding windows. Each menu contains several submenus and some submenus have relevant menu items.

Site menu contains five submenus in all—**Control Panel**, **User Manager**, **Media Manager**, **Global Configuration**, and **Logout**. These submenus are standardized and do not change.

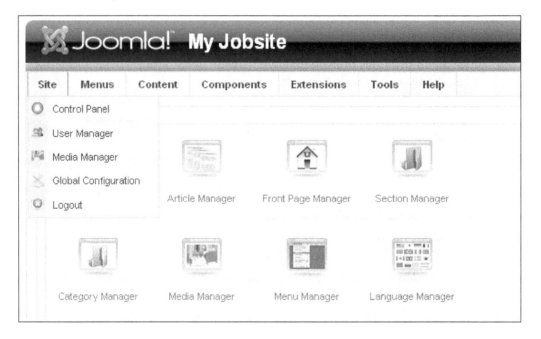

The following table shows the uses of the submenus of **Site** menu:

Submenus	Uses or relevance
Control Panel	Provides links to administrator control panel and returns to default control panel interface.
User Manager	Opens **User Manager** window, which enables you to add new user, edit, or delete existing user. In order to add new user, click on **New** on the top right-hand side of the window and provide related information in all mandatory fields of the next window **User: [New]** and then click on **Save**. If you want to edit or delete any existing user account, first select the account by checking and then clicking on the corresponding buttons.
Media Manager	Opens **Media Manager** window, which provides you the functionality to manage images and other media files. To delete media files from the **Media Manager** window, first check files and then click on the **Delete** button at the top right-hand side of the window. You can also upload files from this window. To do this, select the file (maximum of 10 MB) that you want to upload by clicking on the **Browse** button and then clicking on the **Start Upload** button at the bottom of the window to upload the file.

Submenus	Uses or relevance
Global Configuration	Opens **Global Configuration** window. In this window, you can change settings and configuration of your website. This window has three tabs — **Site**, **System**, and **Server**. Each tab contains several types of settings such as **Site Settings**, **Metadata Settings**, **SEO Settings**, **System Settings**, **User Settings**, **Media Settings**, **Debug Settings**, and so on.
Logout	By using this menu, you can log out from the administrator control panel.

Menus menu is used to control navigation menus of the frontend of the website. By default, this menu contains submenus such as **Menu Manager**, **Menu Trash**, and **Main Menu** or any navigation menu that you have added to your website, which will also be shown here.

The following table shows uses of **Menu Manager**, **Menu Trash**, and **Main Menu** submenus:

Submenus	Uses or relevance
Menu Manager	Opens **Menu Manager** window, which enables you to add a new menu, or edit, or delete any existing menu. In order to add a new menu, click on **New**, provide necessary information in the next window **Menu: [New]**, and then click on **Save**. If you want to edit, copy, or delete a menu, first select the menu by checking it from the list and then click on the corresponding buttons. For example, to edit a menu, click on **Edit**.
Menu Trash	Opens **Menu Trash** window. From this window, you can restore or permanently delete any menu item that you have moved here earlier. You need to check the menu item and then click on either **Restore** or **Delete**, depending on what you want to do.
Main Menu	Controls the default navigation menu layout of the Joomla! website. It opens the relevant menu item manager window. In this window, you will see the list of menu items. These menu items will be displayed on your website front page as a navigation menu. You can add a new menu item and manage the existing menu items in this window. To add new menu items, click on the **New** button on the top, right-hand side of the window and then select a menu item type link in the **Menu Item: [New]** window. After this, provide the information in the next screen and click on **Save**. For example, to add a new menu item for a specific article, you need to click on **Internal Link | Articles | Article Layout** in the **Menu Item: [New]** window. After that, provide the required information and specify the article in the next screen and then click on **Save**.
	If you want to edit, copy, delete, publish, or unpublish any menu item, first check the menu item from the list and then click on the corresponding buttons. For example, click on **Delete** to delete any menu item.

Content menu provides facilities for managing website contents, sections, categories, and front page layout. It has five submenus — **Article Manager**, **Article Trash**, **Section Manager**, **Category Manager**, and **Front Page Manager**.

The following table shows all of the submenus and their uses:

Submenus	Uses or relevance
Article Manager	Opens the **Article Manager** window, which enables you to add a new article, and edit or delete an old article. To add a new article, click on the **New** button on the right-hand side of the window, provide a title and the required information in the new window **Article: [New]**. Now write your article in the editing area of this window and click on **Save**. To manage, that is, edit, copy, move, move to trash, publish, or unpublish any article that is already in your website, first check it from the list and then click on the related buttons.
Article Trash	Opens the **Article Trash** window. From this window, you can restore or permanently delete any article you have moved to trash previously. You need to check the article and then click on either **Restore** or **Delete**, depending on what you need to do.
Section Manager	Opens the **Section Manager** window, which enables you to manage sections. Sections are important to organize similar content in the section. You can easily add a new section or manage existing sections. To add a new section, click on **New**, provide a title for the new section and the required information, and finally click on **Save**. To edit, copy, delete, publish, or unpublish any existing section, first check it from the list and then click on the related buttons.

Submenus	Uses or relevance
Category Manager	Opens the **Category Manager** window. It enables you to manage category. Categories are important to arranging contents in different relevant categories under a specific section. You can easily add a new category or manage categories. To add a new category, click on **New**, provide a title for a new category and other information, and finally click on **Save**. To edit, copy, delete, publish, or unpublish any existing category, first check it from the list and then click on the related buttons.
Front Page Manager	Provides you functionalities to manage the content of your website front page. To remove any article, publish, or unpublish any existing article easily, first check it from the list and then click on the related buttons. For example, to remove any article from publishing on front page click on **Remove**.

By default, **Components** menu has submenus such as **Banners**, **Contacts**, **News Feeds**, **Polls**, **Search**, and **Web Links**. Components that are installed will also be shown on this menu. We have installed Jobs! 1.1.1 component. So a submenu named **Jobs** will also be shown on this menu.

Now let's see the built-in submenus of **Components** menu and their uses in the following table:

Submenus	Uses or relevance
Banners	Has three corresponding menu items: **Banners**, **Clients**, and **Categories**. These menu items provide you the facility to manage your banners, clients, and banner categories. To add a new banner, click on **New** in **Banner Manager** window and then provide detailed information in the **Banner: [New]** window, and finally click on **Save**. Your banner will not be displayed until you set a module for it. How to use the **Banner** module will be discussed later. To edit, copy, delete, publish, or unpublish any existing banner, first check it from the list and then click on the corresponding buttons.
Contacts	Has two menu items — **Contacts** and **Categories**. You can manage your contacts and contact categories easily by using these menu items. To add a new contact, click on **New** and then provide details for the new contact in **Contact: [New]** window, and then click on **Save**. To edit, copy, delete, publish, or unpublish any existing category, first check it from the list and then click on the related buttons.
News Feeds	Like **Contacts** submenu, **News Feeds** submenu also has two menu items, namely **Feeds** and **Categories**. You can use these to manage your news feeds. To add news feed, click on the **New** button of this window, provide feed details in the **News Feed: [New]** window, and then click on **Save**. To edit, copy, delete, publish, or unpublish any existing news feed, first check it from the list and then click on the corresponding buttons.
Polls	Opens **Poll Manager** window, it enables you to add or manage polls. To add a new poll click on the **New** button of this window and then provide poll details and options in the **Poll: [New]** window, and then click on the **Save** button. To edit, copy, delete, publish, or unpublish any existing polls, first check it from the list and then click on the corresponding buttons.
Search	Opens the **Search Statistics** window and shows you what keywords are used as search terms and how many times they were requested. This feature works only when the **Gather Search Statistics** parameter value is set to **Yes**. To enable this feature, click on the **Parameter** and set the parameter value to **Yes**. If you want to clear all search texts, click on the **Reset** button of the **Search Statistics** window.
Web Links	Also has two menu items — **Links** and **Categories**. These menu items help you to add new links or manage an existing hyperlink. To add a new web link, click on **New** and then provide web link details in the **Web Link: [New]** window, and then click on **Save**. To edit, copy, delete, publish, or unpublish an existing web link, first check it from the list and then click on the related buttons.

Extensions menu has five submenus—**Install/Uninstall**, **Module Manager**, **Plugin Manager**, **Template Manager**, and **Language Manager**.

The following table shows all the submenus of **Extensions** menu and their uses:

Submenus	Uses or relevance
Install/Uninstall	This submenu is related to the **Extensions Manager** window; you can install or uninstall any extensions on this window. This window has six tabs—**Install**, **Components**, **Modules**, **Plug-ins**, **Languages**, and **Templates**. The **Install** tab helps the installation of any extension. To do this, click on the **Browse** button and select the extension file, then click on the **Upload file & Install** button. Other tabs are used to uninstall corresponding extensions. For example, you can uninstall components from **the Components** tab. Just check the component you want to uninstall and then click on **Uninstall**.
Module Manager	Opens the **Module Manager** window, which provides the facility to add, enable, disable, edit, or delete modules. To add a new module, click on the **New** button in this window and then check the radio button of a module. For example, you can check the radio button of the **Banner** module. Now click on the **Next** button at the top right-hand side of the toolbar, provide the detailed information in the **Module: [Edit]** window, and then click on **Save**.
	To edit, copy, delete, enable, or disable any existing module, first check it from the list and then click on the corresponding buttons.

Submenus	Uses or relevance
Plug-in Manager	Opens **Plugin Manager** window. You can enable or disable any plugin or edit any plugin information in this window. To enable or disable any plugin, check it from the list and then click on either **Enable** or **Disable** button. If you want to edit **the** information of a plugin, click on **Edit** after checking the plugin. After that, you can change any information you want in the next window and click on **Save** or **Apply**.
Template Manager	Opens the **Template Manager** window. You can make any template your default template in this window. If you want to use any template as your default website template, check the radio button of the template you want to use and click on the **Default** button at the top right-hand side.
Language Manager	Opens the **Language Manager** window. You can choose any language in this window. To use a language as your default website language, check the radio button of the language you want to use and click on **Default**.

Tools menu has six submenus—**Read Messages**, **Write Messages**, **Mass Mail**, **Global Check-in**, **Clean Cache**, and **Purge Expired Cache**.

The following table shows these submenus and their uses:

Submenus	Uses or relevance
Read Messages	Opens the **Private Messaging** window, which enables you to read, delete, and send messages privately. To read a message, just click on the message link. To delete a message, check it from the list and then click on **Delete**. You can also send your message by clicking on **New** in the **Write Private Message** window. Specify the user to whom you are sending the message and write your message. Finally, click on **Send** to send the message.
Write Messages	Opens the **Write Private Message** window. You can write and send private messages in the same way as mentioned above.
Mass Mail	Opens the **Mass Mail** window. You can use this feature to mail many users at a time. Select any user group—**Registered** or **All user groups**—and write your message with subject, and then click on **Send Mail** to send message.
Global Check-in	Helps to check database tables.
Clean Cache	Opens **Cache Manager** window. It has two tabs—**Site** and **Administrator**. The **Site** tab provides the facility to delete cache files at the frontend of the site. On the other hand, the **Administrator** tab provides the facility to delete cache files of the administrator area. To delete cache files from the website, first check it from the list and then click on **Delete**. You can delete cache files of the administrator area in the same way.
Purge Expired Cache	This submenu opens **Cache Manager - Purge Cache Admin** window. It helps to clean expired cache files.

Help menu contains two submenus—**Joomla! Help** and **System Info**.

The following table shows uses of these submenus:

Submenus	Uses or relevance
Joomla! Help	Opens the **Help** window and provides the related Joomla! help resource link.
System Info	Opens the **Information** window. It contains a total of six tabs — **System Information**, **PHP settings**, **Configuration File**, **Directory Permission**, and **PHP information**. These tabs provide information about your system.

Tools

Tools are displayed at the top right-hand side of the windows (such as **Menu Manager**, **User Manager**, **Article Manager**, **Module Manager**, **Template Manager**, and so on) with corresponding icons. Each tool is relevant to a specific task; various tools are used depending on each window.

The following table shows a list of some common tools and their uses.

Tools	Uses or relevance
Publish	Publishes selected elements.
Unpublish	Unpublishes selected elements.
Enable	Enables selected elements.
Disable	Disables selected elements.
New	Adds a new element.
Edit	Opens editing dialog.
Copy	Copies selected elements.
Apply	Saves elements without closing editing window.
Save	Saves elements and closes the editing window.
Move	Moves selected elements such as article, menu item.
Delete	Deletes selected elements.
Close	Closes the window without saving anything.
Cancel	This tool is similar to close tool. You can use this tool to cancel or close the window without saving anything.
Help	Opens online help resources.

Lists

Lists are useful to manage multiple elements with a single click. For example, first check the appropriate checkbox in the lists and then click on any of the tools, such as Enable or Disable, depending on what action you want to take. If you click on the checkbox at the top, all the elements will be selected.

You can filter list elements by typing keywords (that match the elements you are looking for) in the filter textbox at the top left-hand side, and then clicking on **Go**. You can also sort the list by using the following drop-down lists—**Select Section**, **Select Category**, **Select Author**, and **Select State**. These drop-down lists are in line with the filter textbox. You can also control the number of list elements displayed and navigate through the pages.

Dialogs

Some tools are related to corresponding dialogs. Dialogs contain some common tools, such as **Save**, **Apply**, **Close** or **Cancel**, **Help**, and so on. In most dialogs, the main content is usually shown on the left-hand side and the parameters for this element on the right side. For example, clicking on **New** tool from the **Article Manager** window opens the **Article: [New]** dialog. You will see something similar to the following screenshot:

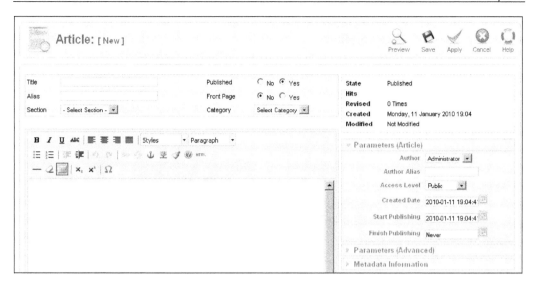

Introducing Jobs! control panel interface

Jobs! Pro and Jobs! Basic, both variations, provide a user-friendly control panel interface. You have full control over your jobsite, and you can manage your site easily by using this control panel.

To go to your Jobs! control panel, click on the menu **Components | Jobs | All Tools**.

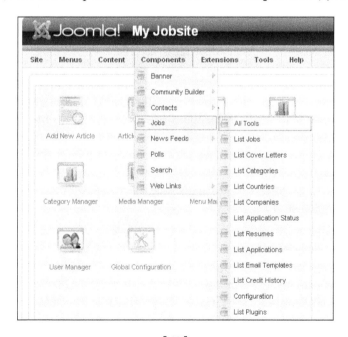

Now, you will see the Jobs! control panel interface. We have installed Jobs! Pro 1.3.2 version. It will look like the following screenshot:

At the top of the screen, you will see all the tabs. You will see all the buttons below these tabs, on the left-hand side. You will see also **RSS Feeds**, **Unpublished Companies**, **Statistics**, and others, beside the buttons on the right-hand side.

Buttons

Buttons are separated into five groups—**Management**, **Job Seeker Tools**, **Employer Tools**, **Credit System**, and **Information**.

Management group contains buttons that are related to jobsite management. There are fourteen buttons in the **Management** group—**Control Panel**, **List Categories**, **List Countries**, **List Application Status**, **List Employers**, **List Job Seekers**, **List Resume Field Categories**, **List Resume Fields**, **List Tools**, **List Education Levels**, **List Job Types**, **List Plugins**, **List Unlock Requests**, and **Settings**.

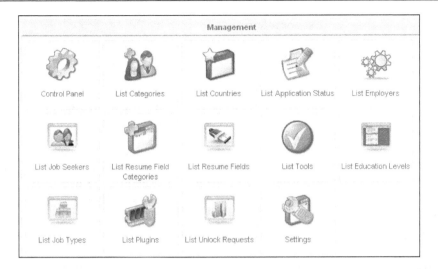

The following table shows the uses of these buttons:

Buttons	Uses or relevance
Control Panel	Returns you to the Jobs! control panel default interface.
List Categories	Opens the **List Categories** window, which provides facilities to manage job categories, such as finance jobs, marketing jobs, technology jobs, and others. These categories are used to classify jobs in their relevant groups. You can easily add new job categories from the **List Categories** window. Click on **Add new category**, provide a category name and other information in the next window, and finally click on **Save** to save it. You can easily edit, publish, unpublish, and delete any category. For this, you need to first check categories in the **List Categories** window and then click on the corresponding buttons.
List Countries	Opens **List Countries** window, which provides the facility to manage countries of the company name. These countries will be displayed as a list and will be used in the **Company Details** section while adding a new company. This helps to identify a company location. For example, if you want to add a company from Bangladesh, you need to add the country Bangladesh in the country list. To add a new country in the list, click on the **Add new country** tool in the **List Countries** window. Now, provide a country name in the **Company Country** field of the next window and save it. You can easily edit, publish, unpublish, or delete a country name. First check the countries in the **List Countries** window and then click on the relevant buttons.

Buttons	Uses or relevance
List Application Status	Opens the **List Application Status** window. You can manage application status in this window. When an application is received from a candidate, application status defines whether the application is accepted or declined. You can add any application-status name on your jobsite such as approved, pending, rejected, and so on. To add a new application status name from the admin panel, click on the **Add new status** button in the **List Application Status** window. You need to provide a status name in the next window and then save it. You can easily edit and delete any application status name. First check application statuses in the **List Application Status** window and then click on the relevant buttons.
List Employers	Opens the **List Employers** window, which provides the facility to view the information of registered employers.
List Job Seekers	Opens the **List Job Seekers** window. You can view information of registered job seekers in this window.
List Resume Field Categories	Opens the **List Resume Field Categories** window, which enables you to manage resume field categories. Resume fields are used to collect certain information to create jobseekers' resumes, and resume field categories categorize resume fields in different groups.
List Resume Fields	Opens the **List Resume Fields** window, where you can define which fields will be used in the resume submission form. Resume fields are used in collecting information from jobseekers.
List Tools	Opens the **List Tools** window, which provides the facility to check and delete unstable records from your Jobs! database tables. When you delete any record, other records that are related to this record are also affected and become unstable. For example:

- You have a user with username 'Sourav'
- You have added two companies against this username
- The user posted some jobs for both the companies
- Each job has received five or more applications
- The user has sent an e-mail to every applicant

If you delete the username 'Sourav' from Joomla! User Manager, all the records related to user 'Sourav' become unstable records. You should delete these unstable records from the database by using **List Tools** window. To do this, click on the link **Check Unstable Records** of the **List Tools** window.

Buttons	Uses or relevance
List Education Levels	Opens the **List Education Levels** window, which provides the facility to manage education levels. Education levels are used in resume submission form to show levels of jobseekers' education. For example, bachelor's degree, master's degree, doctorate degree, and so on. You can add new educational levels and manage others from the **List Education Levels** window.
List Job Types	Opens the **List Job Types** window, which provides the facility to manage job types. Job types define the types of available job positions. For example, temporary, part-time, full-time, internship, and so on. To add a new job type from admin panel, click on the **Add New Job Type** button in the **List Job Types** window. You need to provide a name of job type in the next window and then save it. You can easily edit and delete any job type. First check the job types in the **List Job Types** window and then click on the relevant buttons.
List Plugins	Jobs! Pro has its own plugin system. This button opens **List Plugins** window, which provides the facility to manage Jobs! plugins. For example, Jobs! Prevent Direct Contact, Create Automatic Meta Description, Paypal, Google Checkout, Bank Transfer (or Offline Payment), Jobs! System Debug, and others. You can install them from this window. Select the plugin installer package by clicking on the **Browse** button and then clicking on the **Install** button. You can easily edit, delete, publish, or unpublish any plugin. First check the plugins on the **List Plugins** window and then click on the relevant buttons.
List Unlock Requests	Opens the **List Unlock Requests** window, which provides the facility to approve or reject unlock requests. This is a unique feature of Jobs! Pro. There is a plugin called `lknHideResumeFields`. This plugin can hide selected resume fields from the employers (such as e-mail, phone, contact details, and others). This plugin can hide the selected field completely, or can show a link to the employer to send a request to the site owner to see the field value. If an option is chosen to show the link, the employer is able to send a request to the site owner to see the value of the field. The unlock request lists the resumes and the hidden fields that an employer has requested to see.
	If the plugin is not activated or no field is selected, Jobs! Pro will show all the field values of the resume.
Settings	Opens the **Settings** window. In this window, you can change several settings such as **General Settings**, **Email**, **Job Posting**, **Image**, **Templates**, **Home Page**, **Social Book marking**, **Thank you message**, **Credit System**, and others. You will learn more details in *Chapter 4, Changing Configuration Settings*.

Job Seeker Tools group contains four buttons—**List Cover Letters**, **List Resumes**, **List Resume Files**, and **List Job Alerts**. These buttons are related to the management of jobseekers.

The following table shows the uses of these buttons:

Buttons	Uses or relevance
List Cover Letters	Opens the **List Cover Letters** window, which provides the facility to manage cover letters of all jobseekers. Cover letters are used as applications when jobseekers apply for a job. You can easily add new cover letter, edit, publish, unpublish, or delete any cover letter for a specific jobseeker. First check the cover letter on the **List Cover Letters** window and then click on the relevant buttons.
List Resumes	Opens the **List Resumes** window. You can manage information of jobseekers' resumes in this window. To add a new resume, click on the **Add resume** tool, provide company information in the next window, and save it. You can edit, publish, unpublish, and delete resumes of any jobseeker. First check the resume in the **List Resumes** window and then click on the relevant buttons. For example, click on the **Edit** button to edit a resume.
List Resume Files	Opens the **List Resume Files** window, which enables you to manage resume files uploaded by jobseekers. These resume files will be automatically included with the jobseekers' main resumes.
List Job Alerts	Opens the **List Job Alerts** window, which enables you to manage job alerts. This is a new feature in Jobs! and available only in the Jobs! Pro variation. If a jobseeker adds any job alert, he or she gets a job e-mail, based on his or her job alerts selection criteria. This is one of the best ways to bring back jobseekers to your jobsite.

Employer Tools group contains five buttons—**List Jobs**, **List Companies**, **List Applications**, **List Email Templates**, and **Search Our Resume Database**. These buttons are related to the management of employers.

The following table shows the uses of these buttons:

Buttons	Uses or relevance
List Jobs	Opens the **List Jobs** window. You can add new jobs and manage any job here. To add a new job from the admin panel, open the **List Jobs** window and then click on the **Add New Job** tool of this window. This tool is related to the **Add New Job** window. When the window opens, you may need to provide some mandatory information and then click on the **Save** tool. If you want to edit, delete, publish, or unpublish any job, first check the job on the **List Jobs** window and then click on the corresponding buttons.
List Companies	Opens the **List Companies** window, which provides the facility to manage companies of your clients. To add a new company, click on the **Add new company** tool, provide company information in the next window, and save it. You can also edit, delete, publish, or unpublish any existing company. First check the company in the **List Companies** window and then click on the corresponding buttons.
List Applications	Opens the **List Applications** window, which provides the facility to manage applications received from candidates.
List Email Templates	Opens the **List Email Templates** window. You can manage e-mail templates added by your employers. E-mail templates will be used to send messages to the jobseeker while responding to an application. It helps to save the time and effort of writing a message.
Search Our Resume Database	Opens the **Search Our Resume Database** window, which provides the facility to search the database of the jobseekers' resumes with different criteria.

Credit System group is relevant to managing the user's credit system. The user credit system is the power of an employer to post a new job and use other services. The user will not be able to use services if they have no credit stock in their account. You can charge the user a specific amount of money for purchasing the necessary credit. This section contains two buttons—**List Credit History** and **List Pending Credits**.

The following table shows the uses of these buttons:

Buttons	Uses or relevance
List Credit History	Opens the **List Users Credits** window. You can add new credit or edit existing credits for a specific employer in this window. The greater the number of credits means more power to the employer to use job-posting services and resume database search facilities. The credit system controls and limits the power of job posting. For example, if you provide an employer with 10 credits, he or she will not be able to post more than 10 jobs. You can also fix the expiry date of the resume database search facility for a specific employer.
List Pending Credits	Opens the **List Pending Credits** window; you can approve the pending credits in this window.

Information group provides information of Jobs! component. This section contains three buttons—**Support**, **Credits**, and **License**.

The following table shows the uses of these buttons:

Buttons	Uses or relevance
Support	Helps to view online-support resources.
Credits	Displays developer information.
License	Displays license agreement.

Tabs

Tabs are shown at the top of the screen and almost all tabs are an alternative for buttons. They are linked with similar windows to buttons. For example, the **List Jobs** tabs and **List Jobs** buttons both open the **List Jobs** window. In the Jobs! control panel, you will find the following tabs: **All Tools, List Jobs, List Cover Letters, List Categories, List Countries, List Companies, List Application Status, List Resumes, List Applications, List Email Templates, List Credit History, Configuration, License**, and **List Plugins**.

All Tools	List Jobs	List Cover Letters	List Categories	List Countries	List Companies	List Application Status	List Resumes
List Applications	List Email Templates	List Credit History	Configuration	List Plugins			

The table below shows their uses or relevance.

Tabs	Uses or Relevance
All Tools	This tab is similar to the **Control Panel** button. **Returns to Jobs!** control panel **default interface.**
List Jobs	Opens the **List Jobs** window by which you can add new jobs and manage existing jobs.
List Cover Letters	Opens the **List Cover Letters** window, which helps to manage cover letters.
List Categories	Opens the **List Categories** window, which enables you to manage job categories.
List Countries	Opens the **List Countries** window, which enables you to manage company countries.
List Companies	Opens the **List Companies** window, which enables you to manage employer's companies.
List Application Status	Opens the **List Application Status** window, which helps to manage application status names.
List Resumes	Opens the **List Resumes** window; it helps to manage jobseekers' resume details.

Tabs	Uses or Relevance
List Applications	Opens the **List Applications** window, which helps to manage applications received from a candidate.
List Email Templates	Opens the **List Email Templates** window, which helps to manage e-mail templates.
List Credit History	Opens the **List Credit History** window. You can add new credit or edit existing credit.
Configuration	Opens the **Configuration** window. You can change Jobs! configuration on this window.
License	You can use this tab to see license agreement.
List Plugins	Opens the **List Plugins** window. You can install your Jobs! plugins from this window.

Tools

Like Joomla! 1.5 administrator panel, tools of Jobs! control panel are also displayed on the right-hand side of the managerial windows with the corresponding icons, and each tool is related to a specific task.

The following table shows a list of some popular tools of Jobs! component and their relevance.

Tools	Uses or relevance
Publish	Publishes selected elements.
Unpublish	Unpublishes selected elements.
Edit	Opens editing dialogs.
Delete	Deletes selected elements.
Control Panel	Returns to Jobs! control panel interface back.

Summary

Now, after finishing this chapter, you are able to administrate and run your Joomla! jobsite with ease. This chapter introduced you to the Joomla! 1.5 administrator panel and Jobs! control panel interface. In the next chapter, you will learn the basics of designing a template for your jobsite.

3
Designing a Jobsite Template

You may want to change the design and appearance of your Joomla! 1.5 jobsite. You can easily do this by changing the default template. There are lots of websites (for example: www.123webdesign.com and www.joomlart.com), where you can get templates absolutely free or with a commercial license. You can use any of these templates for your jobsite or you can design your own.

In this chapter, you will learn:

- The basic structure and layout of a template
- Background and color schemes, menus, and interactive buttons
- Template parameters, template reference, and so on
- Coding
- Template installation and testing
- W3C Validation, XHTML validation, CSS validation, and so on

Introduction

Template design involves several tasks and you should have some basic knowledge of website design. You don't need to have a complete understanding of web design technology, but you need an overall appreciation of some basic techniques like: XHTML, CSS, XML, and PHP. The w3school website, http://www.w3schools.com/, is one of the best online resources, for beginners, for learning these techniques. To start designing a template for your Joomla! 1.5 jobsite, first you need to draw a basic structure and layout in Adobe Photoshop, GIMP, or other image editors depending on the look you want to apply to your site. Then you have to start the coding of your template in Notepad or any other text editor. During the coding process, you may need to use background and color schemes on style elements of code. You also need to use some important elements of the Joomla! template reference in your code for the title, metadata, contents, and almost everything about your Joomla! site.

After creating your template, you can use W3C validation services to confirm that your template is compliant with the W3C standards and specifications.

The basic structure and layout of a template

Before you draw a basic structure and layout of the template, you have to decide what elements will be shown on your site and which modules to use. If you want to use only the Jobs! modules and some built-in Joomla modules such as **Main Menu**, **Banners**, **Login Form**, and so on, you can make a basic structure like the following for your template:

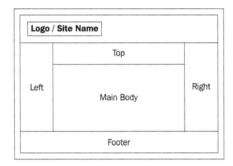

Background and color schemes

To specify a color, especially background color, in your stylesheet, you must be familiar with using colors. There are two main ways to specify colors in your stylesheets: with a predefined color name (such as black, white, and so on), or RGB color value (such as #000000, #ffffff, and so on).

The color names are easy to use and can be placed as the value of any property that is related to color. For example:

```
Color:   black;
```

Color names are limited, so web designers most often use RGB color values instead of color names:

```
Color: #333333;
```

With the background-color property, you can apply background colors to any element. For example:

```
Background-color: #ffffff;
```

Template reference

Generally, any website consists of three types of web pages: the homepage, intermediate pages, and the content page. It may take time and large development efforts to make such a website, but we are making a template for a Joomla!-based jobsite. So we needn't worry! We just need to follow the Joomla! template reference. This method is a shortcut for inserting information, components, modules, and so on.

Jdoc include tags

The jdoc include (`<jdoc:include>`) tags are new to Joomla! 1.5 templates and help to display content specific to the page being viewed. These tags are very easy to use. The most frequently used jdoc include tag types are the following: head, component, installation, and module position.

The head include tag

This is a simple jdoc include tag; this tag contains the information of character encoding type, title and metadata, and so on. By inserting this tag, you can include the information of the head section in your template:

```
<jdoc:include type="head" />
```

The component include tag

The component include tag renders the main content of the page:

```
<jdoc:include type="component" />
```

After inserting this tag, you will see articles, contact forms, and polls, among others on your pages, depending on what components are linked to a specific navigation menu. By default, this statement will load the component that corresponds to the default navigation menu; typically, this is the **Home** menu, which loads the frontpage component. You can also link to any specific component using menu links.

Module position include tag

Module positions define the place of modules in a template and help to display the output from modules assigned to a specific position. The designer has full control over module positions. You can define module positions by inserting the module position include tag. This tag provides you the ability to display modules that are enabled in different parts of your website:

```
<jdoc:include type="modules" name="position" style="styleName" />
```

In the module position include tag, you can apply any one of the following styles:

Style Name	Use or Relevance
None	This style displays a module without title and uses no style.
XHTML	This style displays modules wrapped in a single <div> tag and shows the module titles in <h3> heading elements.
Rounded	This style displays modules with more complex CSS styles and rounded corners.
Table	This style displays modules in a table with a single row column.
Horiz	This style displays modules horizontally in a table with multiple column rows.
Outline	This style is used to preview modules and shows help tips.

Coding

To make your jobsite template, first create a temporary folder with the name jobsitetemplate or you can also define this folder with a different name. Your template files will be created on this folder.

Now, you also have to create a file with the name index.php. Then add the following code on the file:

```
<!DOCTYPE html PUBLIC "-//W3C//DTD XHTML 1.0 Transitional//EN"
"http://www.w3.org/TR/xhtml1/DTD/xhtml1-transitional.dtd">
<html xmlns="http://www.w3.org/1999/xhtml" xml:lang="<?php echo $this-
>language; ?>" lang="<?php echo $this->language; ?>" >
<head>
<jdoc:include type="head" />
</head>
```

This code has started with a DOCTYPE declaration and an <html> tag, and then a jdoc include tag, <jdoc:include type="head"/>, is placed to use header contents (such as title, metadata, and so on).

This is not a complete code. Only the head section has been placed; we have to place the body section too:

```
<body>
  <jdoc:include type="component" />
  </body>
</html>
```

The jdoc include tag, `<jdoc:include type="component"/>`, displays contents. Now, this code has been completed according to the XHTML specification. But this document is static, as no style has been applied and no module has been used.

Now make some changes in the `index.php` page and write the following code in the body section, instead of the jdoc include tag for component:

```
<div id="container">
<div id="header">My Jobsite</div>
<div id="top">
<jdoc:include type="modules" name="top" />
</div>
<div id="content">
<jdoc:include type="component" />
</div>
<div id="left_side">
<jdoc:include type="modules" name="left"/>
</div>
<div id="right_side">
<jdoc:include type="modules" name="right"/>
 </div>
<div id="footer">
<jdoc:include type="modules" name="footer"/>
</div>
</div>
```

In the previous code, four module positions — top, left, right, and footer — have been defined by the jdoc include tag: `<jdoc:include type="modules"/>`. Now you will see that all the elements are placed between the `<div>` tags. The `<div>` tag defines a division in an XHTML document and is often used to group block elements to format them with styles. In the code, you will also see that each `<div>` tag contains an ID attribute. These `<div>` tags are the children of a parent `<div>` tag that contains the attribute `id="container"`.

Later, we will use a stylesheet to control the appearance and layout of this page.

Now take a look at the whole `index.php` page:

```
<!DOCTYPE html PUBLIC "-//W3C//DTD XHTML 1.0 Transitional//EN"
"http://www.w3.org/TR/xhtml1/DTD/xhtml1-transitional.dtd">
<html xmlns="http://www.w3.org/1999/xhtml" xml:lang="<?php echo $this-
>language; ?>" lang="<?php echo $this->language; ?>" >
<head>
<jdoc:include type="head" />
</head>
<body>
```

```
<div id="container">
<div id="header">My Jobsite</div>
<div id="top">
<jdoc:include type="modules" name="top" />
</div>
<div id="content">
<jdoc:include type="component" />
</div>
<div id="left_side">
<jdoc:include type="modules" name="left" />
 </div>
<div id="right_side">
<jdoc:include type="modules" name="right" />
 </div>
<div id="footer">
<jdoc:include type="modules" name="footer" />
</div>
</div>
</body>
</html>
```

This means we have completed the `index.php` page. Now we have to create a stylesheet to control its look and appearance. Before adding the stylesheet, we must check the basic structure and layout of the template we have drawn previously. Then create a new folder with the name `css`. Now make a stylesheet file, `style.css`, on this folder and write the following code on the file:

```
body {
    font-family: Arial, Helvetica, sans-serif;
    margin: 0px;
    padding: 0px;
}
a:link, a:visited {
    text-decoration: underline;
    font-weight: normal;
    color: #ffffff;
    outline: none;
    text-align: left;
}
img {
     border: 0;
}
#header {
    font-size: 36px;
    font-weight: bold;
```

```
        height: 75px;
        padding: 10px;
        background: #000000;
        color: #ffffff;
    }
#top {
margin-left:180px;
margin-right:180px;
    }
#container {
        margin: auto;
        background-color: #669900;
        border: 1px solid #C0C0C0;
        text-align: justify;
        font-size: 12px;
    }
#content {
margin-left:180px;
margin-right:180px;
    }
#left_side {
        position: absolute;
        top: 100px;
        left: 0px;
        width: 160px;
        padding: 0px;
    }
#right_side {
        position: absolute;
        top: 100px;
        right: 0px;
        width:160px;
        padding: 0px;
        }
#footer {
        padding: 25px;
        background-color:#000000;
        font-weight: normal;
        color: #cccccc;

    }
```

In the previous code, first we have declared fonts, margin, and padding in the selector body for the template page's index.php. Then we have specified a declaration (with the properties) of other selectors. The ID selector uses the ID attribute of the XHTML element and is defined with the # symbol.

After completion, save the style.css file. To link it with the index.php page, first open the index.php page and then write the following code in the head section:

```
<link href="<?php echo $this->baseurl ?>/templates/jobsitetemplate/
css/style.css" type="text/css" rel="stylesheet">
```

Next we have to create an XML file with the name templateDetails.xml in the folder jobsitetemplate. This is the installer file and contains all the information regarding the template. We can't install or use the template in Joomla! without this XML file.

You should start it with the following code, which defines XML specification and makes the code readable to parser:

```
<?xml version="1.0" encoding="utf-8"?>
<!DOCTYPE install PUBLIC "-//Joomla! 1.5//DTD template 1.0//EN"
"http://www.joomla.org/xml/dtd/1.5/template-install.dtd">
```

On the next line, you have to define the version of Joomla! you are using:

```
<install version="1.5" type="template">
```

Now define a name for your template such as the following:

```
<name>Jobsite Template</name>
```

You may also define the version of your template:

```
<version>1.0.0</version>
```

And the date of template creation:

```
<creationDate>30 June 2010</creationDate>
```

Then add your name with the author tag, which will indicate that you are the creator of this template:

```
<author>Santonu Kumar Dhar</author>
```

You can include your e-mail address:

```
<authorEmail>santonudhar@gmail.com</authorEmail>
```

You can include your web address too:

```
<authorUrl>www.shinyjobs.net</authorUrl>
```

You can also add your copyright notice, such as the following:

```
<copyright>2010 (c) Santonu Kumar Dhar </copyright>
```

Then, also define the types of license:

```
<license>Creative Common</license>
```

Now create a short description of the template:

```
<description>A simple template, designed by Santonu</description>
```

And define all the files and file locations that are involved with this template:

```
<files>
    <filename>index.php</filename>
     <filename>css/style.css</filename>
    <filename>templateDetails.xml</filename>
</files>
```

You also have to define the positions of template, which have been used:

```
<positions>
            <position>left</position>
            <position>right</position>
            <position>top</position>
            <position>footer</position>
    </positions>
```

Then add the `</install>` tag, save the file, and look at the `templateDetails` `.xml` page:

```
<?xml version="1.0" encoding="utf-8"?>
<!DOCTYPE install PUBLIC "-//Joomla! 1.5//DTD template 1.0//EN"
"http://www.joomla.org/xml/dtd/1.5/template-install.dtd">
      <install version="1.5" type="template">
        <name>jobsitetemplate</name>
        <version>1.0.0</version>
    <creationDate>30 June 2010</creationDate>
    <author>Santonu Kumar Dhar</author>
        <authorEmail>santonudhar@gmail.com</authorEmail>
        <authorUrl>www.shinyjobs.net</authorUrl>
     <copyright>2009 (c) Santonu Kumar Dhar </copyright>
    <license> Creative Common</license>
```

```
<description>Simple Joomla Template, Design by Santonu</description>
  <files>
          <filename>index.php</filename>
              <filename>css/style.css</filename>
          <filename>templateDetails.xml</filename>
  </files>
      <positions>
              <position>left</position>
              <position>right</position>
              <position>top</position>
              <position>footer</position>
      </positions>
</install>
```

The page `templateDetails.xml` is also complete.

Now look at the `jobsitetemplate` folder; we have created two files: `index.php` and `templateDetails.xml`. We have also created a sub-folder `css` and placed an external stylesheet file, `style.css`, on this.

The folder structure is:

```
Templates\templatename\
index.php
templateDetails.xml
Templates\templatename\css
style.css
```

Then you have to compress the `jobsitetemplate` folder with the `.zip` extension.

Template parameters

You can also define parameters to control the behavior of your template as a super administrator. Template parameters are declared in `templateDetails.xml`. Parameter default values can be set in `params.ini`, which is also referenced in `templateDetails.XML` as a template `<file>`. This element takes a number of arguments, for example, type, name, default, description, and label, which depend on the types of parameters.

You can easily define a template parameter: add a `<param>` element for each parameter that you want to define and insert these between `<params>...</params>` tags. Place this at the bottom of the `templateDetails.xml` and before closing the `</install>` tag.

For example:

```
<?xml version="1.0" encoding="utf-8"?>
<!DOCTYPE install PUBLIC "-//Joomla! 1.5//DTD template 1.0//EN"
"http://www.joomla.org/xml/dtd/1.5/template-install.dtd">
      <install version="1.5" type="template">
        <name>jobsitetemplate</name>
         <version>1.0.0</version>
    <creationDate>30 June 2010</creationDate>
    <author>Santonu Kumar Dhar</author>
        <authorEmail>santonudhar@gmail.com</authorEmail>
        <authorUrl>www.shinyjobs.net</authorUrl>
     <copyright>2009 (c) Santonu Kumar Dhar </copyright>
    <license> Creative Common</license>
  <description>Simple Joomla Template, Design by Santonu</description>
    <files>
            <filename>index.php</filename>
                <filename>css/style.css</filename>
            <filename>templateDetails.xml</filename>
    </files>
        <positions>
                <position>left</position>
                <position>right</position>
                <position>top</position>
                <position>footer</position>
          </positions>
<params>
<param name="myParam" type="text" default=" "
label="What is your site name?" description="" size="25" />
</params>
</install>
```

The earlier example adds a parameter, `"What is your site name?"`, to your template. After adding any parameter, you need to update the ZIP file again.

Installing your template

You can easily install your template on the Joomla! jobsite. You can install the template like any other extension. For example, first click on the **Extensions** menu and then click on the submenu **Install/Uninstall** to open the **Extension Manager** window.

In this window, click on the **Browse** button in the **Upload Package File** area and then select the **Upload File & Install** button.

Your template will be installed. You can also install it from any directory and URL. Just define the location of the package and then click on the **Install** button. If you get an error during installation, you can visit the following webpage: http://www.joomlatutorials.com/joomla-tips-and-tricks/39-joomla-templating/88-joomla-template-installation-and-troubleshooting.html.

Testing

Testing is a very important phase. Testing is the process of demonstrating that errors are not present. There are many approaches to testing. But we will test only whether the template is working properly or not and that the template is satisfying our specification. To do this, you need to assign this template as a default template to your jobsite.

To make this template the default, click on the **Extensions | Template Manager** menu to open the **Template Manager** window and manage templates:

In the window, **Template Manager**, select the radio button in front of the name of the desired template and click on the **Default** icon in the menu bar. A star will be shown beside the selected template as shown in the following screenshot.

Now, switch to your website and click on the **Preview** button in the browser. You may see a different look to your jobsite. You should ensure that there is no error with your template. If everything is okay, then your testing phase is complete. Finally, we need to validate our site to confirm that the jobsite template is created according to the W3C standards.

Validating W3C

The Markup Validation Services by the **World Wide Web Consortium** (**W3C**) allows users to check XHTML and CSS documents for conformance to XHTML or CSS standards. You should validate your website for the following reasons:

- Validation eases maintenance
- It works as a debugging tool
- It also provides a facility for future-proof quality check
- It helps teach good practices
- It is a sign of professionalism

XHTML validation

Now, we have to ensure that our template is W3C validated, but first we will check the XHTML standard. We have used XHTML coding in the `index.php` file along with the PHP script. But the web browser will display only XHTML codes. So we need to validate the page to confirm that it is bug-free and created properly according to W3C specifications. To validate any website, first go to the W3C XHTML validation page: `http://validator.w3.org/`. There are three options for validating a document with W3C standard: **Validate by URI**, **Validate by File Upload**, and **Validate by Direct Input.** If your site is in the offline mode, then you can choose the second or third option. But if your site exists online, then you can chose the first one.

To validate your jobsite template by URI, type the URL of your jobsite in the **Address** field and then click on the **Check** button.

After validating successfully, your template you will show an output like the following:

CSS validation

You can also validate the CSS file, style.css file, or other stylesheet files if you have linked with index.php page in the same way. To validate your CSS document, go to W3C CSS validation page, `http://jigsaw.w3.org/css-validator/`, and then type the URL of your site in the **Address** field and click on the **Check** button. You'll probably see an output like the following after validating your template successfully.

Summary

The template has always been one of Joomla's most powerful features. This chapter explained the basics of creating a Joomla! 1.5 template. You can aspire to learn a great deal. After finishing this chapter, you will have a clear understanding of the Joomla! 1.5 template designing basics.

4
Changing Configuration Settings

In Joomla! 1.5, the configuration settings feature as **Global Configuration,** which controls most of the operations of the site. The component Jobs! Pro 1.3.2 also has its own configuration settings feature. In order to apply your settings to your jobsite, you need to use both features. By changing the configuration settings of Joomla! 1.5 and Jobs! Pro 1.3.2, you can control your site and adapt it for your jobsite project.

This chapter includes:

- Joomla! 1.5 Global Configuration
- Introducing the Site tab
- Introducing the System tab
- Changing the configuration settings for Jobs! Pro 1.3.2

Introduction

In the **Global Configuration** window, you can change the site name, metadata, SEO settings, user settings, database settings, and so on. This feature provides the facility to manage all of the settings that are needed to control your Joomla! website. On the other hand, Jobs! Pro 1.3.2 configuration enables you to control your component settings, which are essential to work the jobsite properly.

Joomla! 1.5 Global Configuration

Global Configuration is the most important feature of Joomla! 1.5. This feature is related to the configuration.php file. After logging into your Joomla! admin panel, click on **Site | Global Configuration** to open the **Global Configuration** window. In the **Global Configuration** window, you can see three tabs: **Site**, **System**, and **Server**.

Introducing the Site tab

The **Site** tab is directly related to the website and provides the facility to change the basic information on the website. This tab contains three main features: **Site Settings**, **Metadata Settings**, and **SEO Settings**.

Site Settings

Site Settings is one of the main features of Global Configuration, which enables you to change the site title, and controls the availability of the website. This feature includes the following settings:

- **Site Offline**: This setting has two options—**No** and **Yes**. By default, the option is **No**. Select the value **Yes** if you want to make your site temporarily unavailable online.

- **Offline Message**: This message will be displayed when the site is unavailable online. You can change the default message.

- **Site Name**: Type your site name in this field. For example, **My Jobsite**.

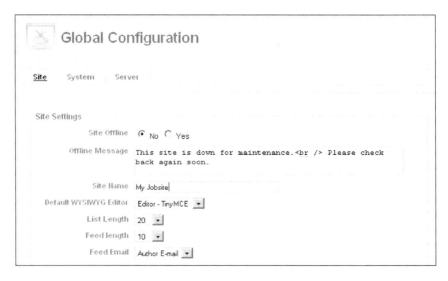

- **Default WYSIWYG Editor**: WYSIWYG stands for What You See Is What You Get and the default editor selection is **Tiny MCE**. You can also choose the **No Editor** option from the list if you do not want to use the WYSIWYG editor.

- **List Length**: This field sets the default length of lists in the control panel for all users. You can select any number in the drop-down list; by default, this is set to **20**.

- **Feed Length**: This field is set to show the number of content items in a specific feed. Select the number of items you want to show in a feed; by default, this is set to **10**.

Metadata Settings

The **Metadata Settings** provide the facility to change the meta information of your website and contain features such as the following:

- **Global Site Meta Description**: This is used as the meta description of a site. Type a description of your jobsite in this field. For example:

  ```
  Welcome to My jobsite!  -   Job vacancy & employment opportunity
  ```

- **Global Site Meta Keywords**: This is used as the meta keywords of a site. Type your keywords in this field. For example:

  ```
  jobs, hot jobs, top jobs, career, employment, jobsite
  ```

- **Show Title Meta Tag**: This setting controls showing the title meta tag—`<meta name="title">`—with the title description of your article. The default selection is always **Yes**. You should keep the default.

- **Show Author Meta Tag**: This setting is quite similar to the previous one. It enables you to show the author meta tag—`<meta name="author">`—when viewing an article. The default selection is **Yes**. You should keep this default.

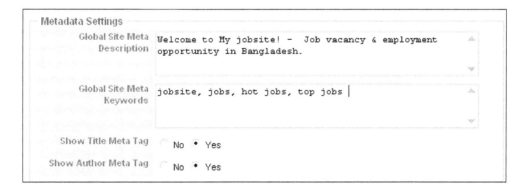

SEO Settings

SEO Settings provide the ability to optimize your jobsite for search engines and include features such as the following:

- Search Engine Friendly URLs: The default selection for this setting is always **No**. To make URLs search engine-friendly, select the option **Yes**. This feature makes URLs clearer and easier to understand by their relevance. The reason for having search engine-friendly URLs is to force related keywords to appear in the URL, which is important to get a best search engine ranking. For example:

    ```
    http://localhost/index.php?option=com_banners&task=click&bid=3
    ```

    This may be encoded as the following:

    ```
    http://localhost/index.php/component/banners/click/3
    ```

- **Use Apache mod_rewrite**: The default selection for this feature is always **No**. So, you will see **index.php** in the URL, for example, `http://localhost/index.php/contact`. If you want to make this URL more search engine-friendly and do not want to display `index.php` in URLs, then you need to select the value **Yes**. Before applying the **Yes** option in this setting, rename the `htaccess.txt` file (can be found in the root directory) to `.htaccess`. But if you don't want to use `mod_rewrite` function, keep this to **No** and don't rename `htaccess.txt`.

- **Add suffix to URLs**: This feature enables you to add the `.html` extension to the end of URLs. The default selection is **No**. Select the value **Yes** if you want to display `.html` extension in the URLs such as the following:
    `http://localhost/index.php/contact.html`.

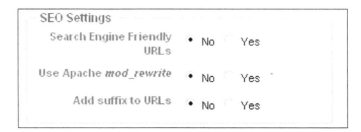

Introducing the System tab

The **System** tab contains features such as **System Settings**, **Users Settings**, **Media Settings**, **Debug Settings**, **Cache Settings**, and **Session Settings**.

System Settings

The **System Settings** involve the following settings:

- **Secret Word**: This is an auto-generated random code for each installation and is used for security reasons. This code cannot be changed.

- **Path to Log folder**: This feature defines the folder or directory location in which the folder log file will be stored.

- **Web Services**: This feature provides the facility to make RPC (Remote Procedure Calls) using HTTP as the transport medium and XML as the encoding language. The default selection for this setting is **Yes**.

- **Help Server**: This setting provides a list of the available help resources in different language options or alternatives. This setting is not important, so you do not need to change this setting; you can leave it at default. The default selection is Joomla!'s main help site, `http://help.joomla.org`.

Users Settings

The **Users Settings** include some important settings such as:

- **Allow User Registration**: The default selection for this setting is **Yes**. Select the option **No** if you do not want to allow the self-registration process of users. That means the user will not be able to register a new user account him/herself.

- **New User Registration Type**: Defines the default access level for new users being registered on the website. There are different user levels with different powers, such as Registered, Author, Editor, and Publisher. The default selection is **Registered**. Registered users have limited access to the site; usually, they can only view website content.

- **New User Account Activation**: When the selected option is **Yes**, an activation link will be sent to new user's e-mail account. The default selection is always **Yes**.

- **Front-end User Parameters**: This setting has two options—**Hide** and **Show**. The default selection for this setting is **Show**. If the selected option is **Show**, users will be able to select their language, article editor, and help site preferences from within their Details screen when they log into the frontend.

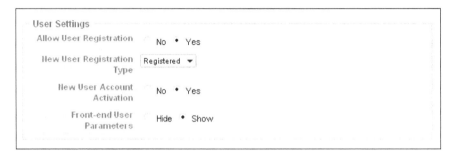

Media Settings

The **Media Settings** are useful to manage any media files. You can control your media files by applying the following settings:

- **Legal Extensions (File Types)**: Here you can define the file types that are allowed to be uploaded by users. By default, the basic image and document files are allowed in Joomla!, such as bmp, csv, doc, epg, gif, ico, jpg, pdf, png, ppt, and txt.

- **Maximum Size (in bytes)**: You can also define the maximum file size, users are allowed to upload, in bytes. The default value is 10000000 bytes (10MB), you can use zero for no limit.

- **Path to Media Folder**: Here you can change the folder where images and other media files will be stored. The default folder is images.

- **Path to Image Folder**: If you want to change the folder where only images used in contents will be stored, you can do so easily by defining a new path. For example, images/sample. The default folder is images/stories.

- **Restrict Uploads**: This feature has two options—**No** and **Yes**. By selecting **Yes**, you can activate uploading restriction for non-managerial user account.

- **Minimum User Level for Media Manager**: Here you can select the lowest user level that will be able to access the media manager in the frontend. You can select any of following—Registered, Author, Editor, and Publisher. The default selection is **Author**. So, Author and its upper user levels, such as Editor and Publisher, will be able to access media manager in the frontend. You should not give access to the Registered users for security reasons—if you are not controlling the user registration process.

- **Check MIME Types**: This uses MIME Magic or File info to verify files. The default selection is **Yes**. You should select **No** if you get any mime type errors.

- **Legal Image Extensions (File Types)**: In this feature, you can allow the image extension types that can be uploaded. These are used to check for valid image headers. By default, Joomla! allows only basic image extensions such as `bmp`, `gif`, `jpg`, `png`.

- **Ignored Extensions**: You can define any extension here, which will be ignored for MIME type checking and restrict uploads. By default, this field is blank.

- **Legal MIME Types**: Here you can define the legal MIME types for uploads. The default values in this field are `image/jpeg, image/gif, image/png, image/bmp, application/x-shockwave-flash, application/msword, application/excel, application/pdf, application/powerpoint, text /plain`, and `application/x-zip`.

- **Illegal MIME Types**: You can also define the illegal MIME types to restrict uploads. By default, `text/html` is restricted to uploading. You should keep this default setting for security reasons.

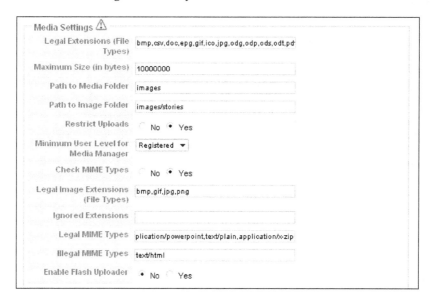

- **Enable Flash Uploader**: This feature is for uploading Flash files in the media manager. Keep this at **No** because this feature will not work properly if any compatible Flash settings are not set by Adobe.

Debug Settings

The **Debug Settings** involve two basic settings: **Debug System** and **Debug Language**.

- **Debug System**: Debug system has two options—**No** and **Yes**. Select the **Yes** option to show the debugging errors in both the frontend and backend.

- **Debug Language**: When the **Yes** option is selected, debug language will work without the **Debug System**. But it will not provide additional detailed references that would help in correcting any errors. Enable this feature only when you want to show the debugging indicators for the language files. It is recommended to always set this value to **No**.

Cache Settings

Cache Settings are used to enable cache files and control cache time. You can control cache files by changing settings such as the following:

- **Cache**: By selecting the **Yes** option here you enable caching. The default selection is **No**. If you enable cache, you need to clear the cache files regularly. So it is recommended to keep this setting to **No**.

- **Cache Time**: Determines the maximum length of time in minutes for a cache file to be stored before it is refreshed. The default setting is **15** minutes.

- **Cache Handler**: There is only one cache handler, which is file-based.

Session Settings

The word session refers to a period of time that has been set aside for some specific purpose or activity. The session settings control how long you will be logged in and able to access the registered user's area. The **Session Settings** include:

- **Session Lifetime**: This setting determines how long a user will be logged in. The default value is **15** minutes.

- **Session Handler**: This setting determines how the session will be handled while users are logged in to the site. The default selection is **Database**.

Server Settings

The **Server Settings** are basic settings that can make an impact. The **Server Settings** are the following:

- **Path to Temp-folder**: You can define a folder to store temporary files and enable write permission.

- **GZIP Page Compression**: The default selection is **No**. Enable it only if compressed buffered output is supported in your server. The advantage is that the page loads faster because the basic rule is that the server provides the data to your browser as a GZIP compresses and it uncompresses when being viewed.

- **Error Reporting**: This enables you to select the level of reporting that is most appropriate. The default selection is **System Default**.

- Force SSL: An SSL (Secure Socket Layer) Certificate establishes a private communication channel enabling encryption of the data during transmission. This encryption provides a facility to log in safely to a website. If any SSL Certificate provided by the trusted **Certificate Authority** (**CA**) is already installed in your server, you can force for using SSL encryption connection in your entire site or administration section only.

Local Settings

Local settings allow you to change your time zone.

- **Time Zone**: You can change your time zone to show current date and time. The default time zone is **(UTC 00:00) Western Europe Time, London, Lisbon, Casablanca**. Select the time zone depending on where you are or where the majority of your visitors live.

FTP Settings

FTP means File Transfer Protocol and it is a method of transferring files from one computer to another conveniently. By changing the FTP setting, you can control the FTP server access.

- **Enable FTP**: If you need to use the FTP layer, you can enable it by selecting the option **Yes**.

- **FTP Host**: If you have enabled FTP, type your FTP server address in this field. For example: `ftp.example.com`.

- **FTP Port**: This field shows the port number that is used to access FTP. The default port is 21.

- **FTP Username**: Type your FTP username in this field.

- **FTP Password**: Type your FTP password in this field.

- **FTP Root**: You can also define the root directory for your FTP server (in which the files will be uploaded).

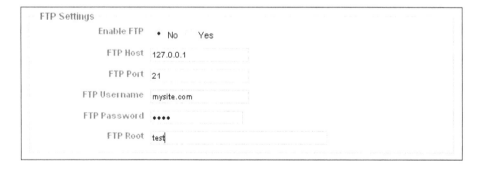

Database Settings

The **Database Settings** allow you to connect your site with a database. This is an initial step and you have already done these settings during your installation. But you can change this anytime. You shouldn't change it without having a knowledge of what you're doing; it may affect your website's functionality completely. The settings involve the following:

- **Database Type**: Define the type of database you are using. By default, the selection is **mysql**. You don't need to change it.

- **Hostname**: Type the address of your database server in this field. In case of local server, type: `http://localhost/`.

- **Username**: Type your database username in this field to access the database. For example: the default username for MySQL database is `root`.

- **Password**: Type your database password in this field.

- **Database**: Type the name of your database in this field.

- **Database Prefix**: Define the prefix that will be used before the names of the database tables. The default prefix is `jos_`. For security reasons, it is beneficial to use a different prefix, but of course, this must be done during installation, or you should change the database tables manually before changing it. Do not change anything if are not sure.

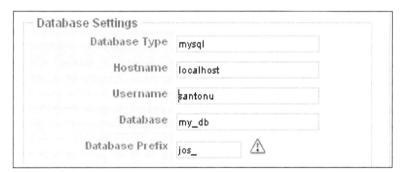

Mail settings

The **Mail Settings** are used to send e-mail messages to users. Do not change anything without knowledge of what you're doing.

- **Mailer**: This setting uses a mailer system to send messages from the site. The default selection is the PHP Mail Function. This is the built-in system for sending messages. You can also select **Sendmail** to use the HTML e-mail forms or SMTP server to use the SMTP server.

- **Mail form**: Type your e-mail address, which will be used to send messages by e-mail forms.

- **From Name**: The site name that you have defined during installation will be displayed in this field. But you can also define any name.

- **Sendmail Path**: This setting indicates the path where the **Sendmail** program is located.

- **SMTP Authentication**: Select **Yes** when the SMTP server requires authentication to send mail.

- **SMTP Username**: Type your SMTP username here to access the server.

- **SMTP Password**: Type your SMTP password here to access the server.

- **SMTP Host**: Type the address of SMTP server here.

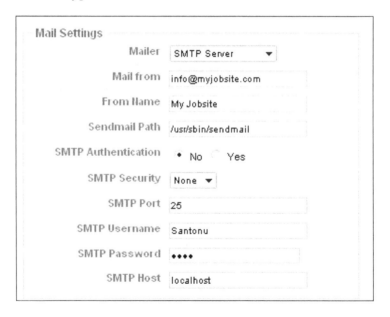

After making changes in the **Global Configuration** window, click on the **Save** button.

Changing Jobs! Pro 1.3.2 Configurations

Jobs! Pro Configuration allows you to change your jobsite settings. To open the Jobs! Pro Configuration window, click on **Components | Jobs | Configuration**. The **Configuration** window involves settings like the following:

General Settings

The **General Settings** tab enables you to change some basic settings, such as:

- **Download ID**: You need to write your DownloadID to validate your installation. If you do not know your DownloadID, go to http://www.instantphp.com/ and log in to your account to edit your license details.

- **Date Format**: You can use the PHP formatting strings as the date format. By default, this is: %d.%m.%Y %H:%M:%S.

- **Records on a page**: You can define how many records will be displayed on a page. By default, the value is 20.

- **Language**: You can select the default language for the Jobs! Pro 1.3.2 Component.

- **Default Status**: This setting shows the default status, which will be used when a user applies for a job.

- **Activate Company functions**: This function enables your users to add their companies and use services like job posting, viewing applicants, resume search, and so on. Select the option **Yes** to activate this function. The default selection is always **Yes**. You must keep the default value **Yes** if you are developing the jobsite only for your own company, and if you do not want to use the company function, then select the option **No**.

- **Activate Job Seeker Functions**: This function enables your users to add their resumes and an online application facility. Select the option **Yes** to activate this function. The default selection is always **Yes**. You must keep the default value **Yes** if you do not want to provide jobseeker services from frontend, and if you want to add the jobseekers' resumes yourself, only in the admin panel, then select the option **No**.

- **Show Toolbar**: This setting has two options — **Show** or **Hide**. Select the option **Show** to show the component toolbar.

- **Category Order**: You can define the job categories by title and ID in an ascending or descending order.

- **Make Jobs! National**: This feature provides you the facility to make your site for a specific country. To do this, you need to add a new country and need to define country ID in the field. How to add a country will be discussed later. If you do not want to use this feature, enter zero (0) in the field.

- **Hide Company**: This setting includes three features—**Show All Company Details**, **Allow Company Choose**, and **Hide All Company Details**. Use or relevance of these features is shown in the table below:

Features	Use or relevance
Show All Company Details	The details of the company will be displayed.
Allow Company Choose	This will be an option for employers to post jobs anonymously.
Hide All Company Details	This option hides company details to users; only applicants can see the details.

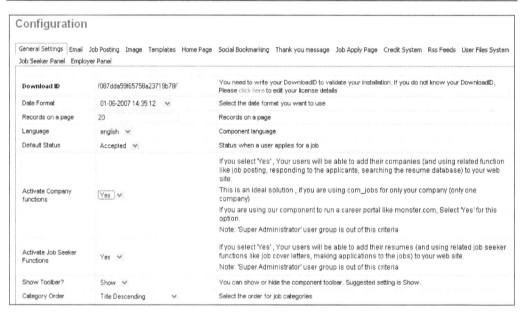

Email

This setting tab is quite similar to the **Email** settings of Joomla! Global Configuration. The e-mail setting includes the following:

- **Mailer**: The default selection is PHP Mail Function. You can also select **Sendmail**, **SMTP server**, and **Gmail**. Although you have already selected a mailer in the Global configuration window for the entire site, you need to specify the mailer function here again.

- **Gmail Username**: If you are using Gmail as the mailer, then type your Gmail username here. For example: `santonudhar@gmail.com`

- **Gmail Password**: Type your Gmail password here to send mail using your Gmail account.

- **Credit Buying**: The default selection is **Yes.** You (the site owner) will get a notification mail when someone buys credit.

- **Adding or updating company**: You will get a notification mail when someone adds or updates the company information. The default selection is always **Yes**.

- **Notification E-Mail**: You can define the email address where the notification emails should be sent.

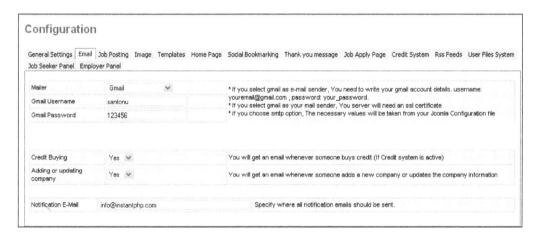

Job posting

This tab enables you to change the following settings:

- **Publish Down Time Editable**: The employers will be able to change the publish down time by using this feature. When this option is enabled, employers will be able to change their job's Start Publishing and Stop Publishing dates. This way they can extend the expiring date at any time from the frontend employer panel. The default selection is **No**. If you do not want to give the power to the employers to change the publishing and expiring date, leave this at default. The employer will not able to edit the publishing and expiring date of any job once he/she has posted the job on the site.

- **Default Publish Down Time**: You can also specify a default publish down time. All jobs will be unpublished when the **Default Publish Down Time** is over. For example, if you specify three months, then any job will be unpublished three months after the posting date.

Image

Employers may upload their company logos or icons. On the other hand, jobseekers will also upload their photographs or other images. So it is important to set some parameters to control these images. You can set them in the image tab of Jobs! Pro configuration. **Image** tab settings include:

- **Logo Image Folder**: You can define the directory location of the Logo image. This directory must exist and the directory location must start and finish with a slash(/). By default, the directory location of the Logo image is /image/ stories/jobs/logos. This directory will be automatically created during the installation of the Jobs! Pro component.

- **Resume Image Folder**: You can also define the directory location for where to store the jobseeker's photographs. By default, the directory location of these images is /images/stories/jobs/cv_images/.

- **Allowed Image Types**: Type the image extension(s) in this field, which are allowed to upload in your jobsite. For example: jpeg, jpg, png, gif.

- **Image Size (KB)**: Indicates the maximum size of the image you can upload.

- **Image Resize Active?**: When you select the option **Yes**, the image resize feature will be active and resume images and company logos will be resized.

- **Watermark Text**: This feature inserts text as watermark on the image. Leave this field blank to disable this feature.

- **Watermark Text Color**: You can specify the color of the watermark text in hexadecimal color code on this field. By default, the value is #000000.

- **Watermark Text Background Color**: You can also specify the background color of the watermark text in the hexadecimal color code on this field. By default, the value is #FFFFFF.

- **Watermark Resume Images**: When the selected option is **Yes**, the watermark text will be displayed in the resume images. The default selection is **Yes**.

- **Resume Images Width**: Indicates the maximum width of resume images. The default value is 100.

- **Resume Images Height**: Indicates the maximum height of resume images. The default value is 160.

- **Watermark Company Logos**: When the selected option is **Yes**, the watermark text will be displayed in the company logos. The default selection is **Yes**.

- **Company Logo Width**: Indicates the maximum width of logos. The default value is 150.

- **Company Logo Height**: Indicates the maximum height of logos. The default value is 40.

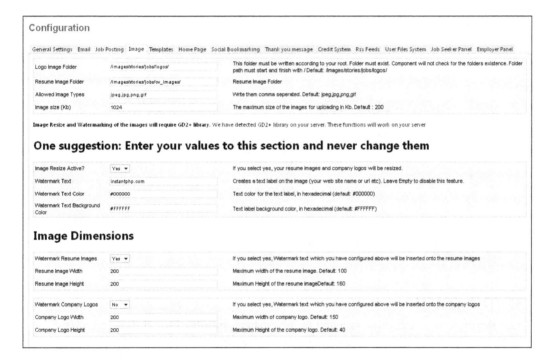

Templates

The **Templates** tab provides the facility to change some settings related to the template:

- **Select The Template**: Select the template of Jobs! Pro component from the list. Leave it at **default** to use the default template.

- **Advice Title**: If you want to show advice for job seekers in the job details page, type the advice title in this field.

- **Advice**: Type your advice for job seekers in this text area.

- **Template Footer**: If you have some knowledge of (X)HTML coding, you can easily edit the template footer. You can also place your copyright information here. If you have no prior knowledge of (X)HTML coding, you should leave it blank.

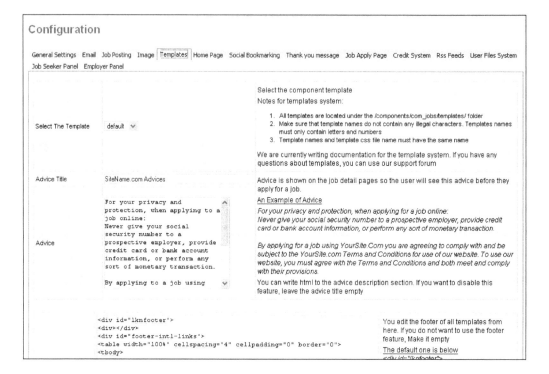

Home page

These settings make effective rules to manage the contents of the default page (for example: `http://localhost/index.php?option=com_jobs`) of the Jobs! Component:

- **Show Job Categories**: If the selected option is **Yes**, job categories will be shown to the default page.

- **Category Column Count**: You can declare here the number of category column(s).

- **Job Counts**: When the selected option is **Show**, the number of jobs for each category will be displayed in the related category.

- **Show Latest Jobs**: You can select the option **Show** to show all the latest jobs. You must install and enable the module **Latest Jobs** before doing this.

- **Indeed Job Roll?**: You can also use Indeed Jobroll modules and be able to show or hide its functionality. The default selection is always **Hide**. Indeed, Jobroll module helps to add Indeed.com site functionalities to your jobsite. Indeed.com is a popular job search engine. It is not a list of message boards or a place where you can actually submit your resume. Indeed searches jobs listed on job boards, newspaper sites, and niche sites. Indeed dynamically monitors job listings on these websites on a continuous basis so that in one simple search you can find the very latest jobs listed on every site.

- **Latest Jobs Count**: Indicates that the number of latest jobs will be shown. By default, it is '10'.

- **Show Simple Search Form**: You can show a simple search form in your jobsite front page.

- **"New to IknJobs?"**: This option provides information about Jobs! component. You can disable this feature by selecting the option **'Hide'**.

- **"Who We Are?"**: This feature enables you to describe your team. The default selection is **'Show'**. Write an article about your job site and link to that article using these. You can disable this feature by selecting the option **'Hide'**.

- **"Ads on home page?"**: You can insert your Google Adsense, Adbrite.com, Clicksor.com, Linkshare.com, CJ.com, or other advertisement service codes here, in HTML and other coding forms.

- **Home Page Companies**: This setting has options, such as **Latest Companies**, **Random Companies**, and **Hide**. If the selected option is **Latest Companies**, then only latest companies will be displayed with a logo on your home page. The option **Random Companies** is the same, but it displays all companies randomly. The option **Hide**, disables this feature.

- **Home Page Company Count**: You can define here how many companies will be shown to your homepage.

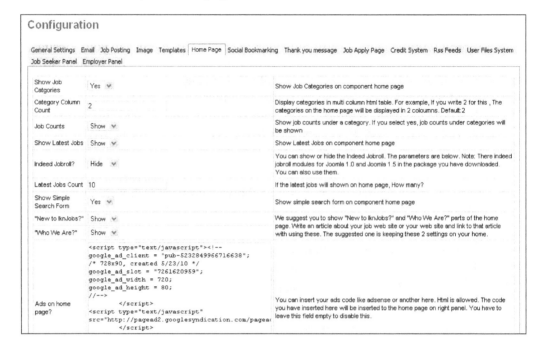

Social Bookmarking

You can easily add the social bookmarking buttons by applying these settings:

- **Social Bookmarking Active?**: If the selected option is **Yes**, the social bookmark button will be displayed in the job details page under the company logo and company link.

- **Button Type**: You can define the button types of social bookmarking. If the selected button is **Local Buttons**, buttons will be displayed from your server. The option **AddThis.com Button** displays buttons from the addthis.com server.

- **AddThis.com ID**: If you have selected the **AddThis.com Button** in the button type above, then write your **AddThis.com ID**. You will get this ID from their website: www.addthis.com.

- **AddThis.com button**: This is a popular website that provides the facility to bookmark any webpage. If you are using the addthis.com button, you can type here the URL of any **AddThis.com** button image. For example: `http://s7.addthis.com/static/btn/lg-share-en.gif`

Thank you message

This setting enables you to display a confirmation message after the success of an online application process.

- **Thank you message**: Type your thank you message here. This message will be displayed after successfully receiving the application. You can use the following parameters in your message:

Parameters	Use or relevance
{ APPLICANT }	Displays the applicant's full name. You can use it as 'Dear { APPLICANT }' and the output will be shown like this: Dear Sourav Das
{JOB_NAME}	Displays the title of the job that the applicant has applied for.
{COMPANY_NAME}	Displays the employer's company name.

Here is an example of a thank you message:

```
Dear {APPLICANT},
Thank You! You have successfully applied for the {JOB_NAME}. Your
application is in the process of being reviewed.
We hope to contact and notify you soon.
Regards,
Santonu Kumar Dhar
President,HR Dept
{COMPANY_NAME}
```

You can also use an image in your message by using the **Image** button at the bottom.

Job Apply Page

- **Create New Resume on Job Apply Page**: Select the value **Yes** if you want to allow job seekers to create a new resume on the **Job Apply Page** while applying for a new job.

- **Login Warning Place**: You can select the value **Job Apply Pages** or **Job Detail Pages** depending on in which of them you want to display a warning message.

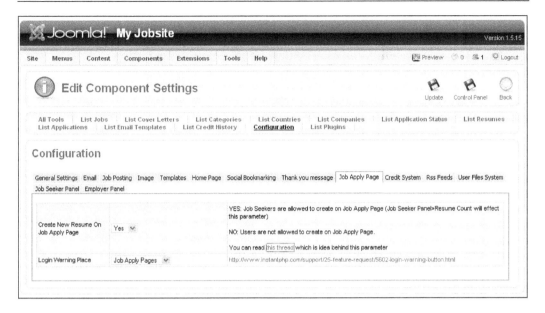

Credit System

The credit system provides the facility to control the credit system. Credit system is a power to users, especially employers, which controls how many jobs they are able to post or how many jobseekers' resumes they can search from the database. If you enable this function for jobseekers also, they will not able to create a resume and apply for new jobs without buying new credits. By using the credit system, you can limit any service and charge them extra money for more credits.

- **One Credit Cost**: Define here the cost of a single credit. If you have defined $0.5 for each credit and your client wants to buy 20 credits, then he/she will be charged $10.

- **Credit System Active for Job seekers?**: The default selection is **No**. If you want to charge jobseekers money for using your services, you can activate the credit system for jobseekers by selecting **Yes**.

- **Creating a Resume Cost**: Write here how many credits adding a resume will cost. For example, if you want to charge a jobseeker for posting a resume, type a value of at least **1**. If you want to provide the jobseeker this service for free, write a zero (0) in the field.

- **Applying a Job Cost**: If you want to charge the jobseeker for applying for a job, in this field, type a value of at least **1**. If you want to provide a jobseeker this service for free, write a zero (0) in the field.

- **Credit System Active?**: Select the option **Yes** to activate the credit system. When the credit system is active, employers will not able to post a new job if their credit limit crosses. The default selection is always **Yes**.

- **Job Cost**: You can also define how many credits a job costs.

- **1 day resume search cost**: Your clients can buy a resume search database with their credits.

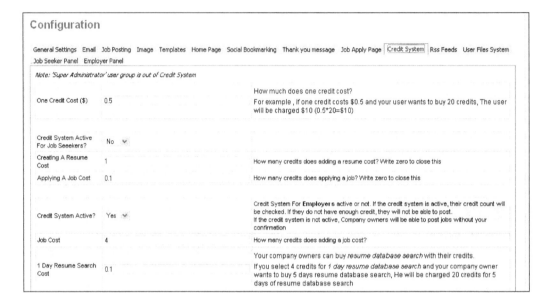

RSS Feeds

RSS is most commonly known as Really Simple Syndication and it is a family of feed formats used to publish frequent updates in a website—such as articles and news headlines—in a standardized format.

You can control the RSS feed setting here. The setting includes:

- **RSS Feeds Active?**: You can enable or disable RSS feeds.

- **Category Feeds?**: This feature enables showing RSS feeds from Categories. If you want to show category feeds, select **Yes**.

- **Company Feeds?**: This feature helps to display RSS feeds from company profiles. If you want to show feeds from the company, select the value **Yes**.

- **Countries Feeds?**: This feature helps to display RSS feeds from Countries. Select the value **Yes** if you want to use this feature.

- **Feed Count**: The default value is **20**. This feature controls how many feeds will be displayed on a page.

- **Limit Job Description**: You can limit the number of characters for job description in feeds. The default value is **300**.

- **How Many?**: How many categories your user can select while creating his/her own feeds.

- **Description**: Write a description of the RSS feed with a maximum of 100 characters.

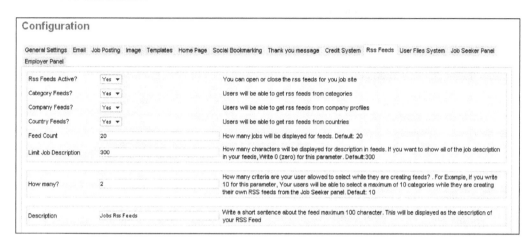

User Files System

The **User Files System** settings enable you to control file system, file types, and file size. This setting includes:

- **UFS Active?**: This feature activates or deactivates the user file system. The user file system helps users, especially jobseekers, to upload and manage their resume and other files.

- **Files Folder**: You can define the directory location of the user file system. This directory must exist and the directory location must start and finish with a slash (/). By default, the directory location of user file system is `/image/stories/jobs/Files`.

- **Allowed Files Types**: Type the file extension(s) in this field, which are allowed to be attached in the resume. For example: `doc`, `pdf`, `zip`, `rar`.

- **Allowed Image Types**: Type the image extension(s) in this field, which are allowed to be attached in the resume. For example: `jpeg`, `jpg`, `png`, `gif`.

- **File Size (KB)**: Indicates the maximum size of file you can upload. The default file size is 1024 KB.

- **Owned File Count**: This feature controls the number of files a user may have. You can omit this feature by using a zero (0).

- **Attach Count**: Indicates the number of files a user can have attached to their resume. You can omit this feature also by using a zero (0).

- **Image Watermark Active?**: When you select the option **Yes**, watermark text features, which you have defined earlier in the **Email** tab, will be activated and inserted in the user files.

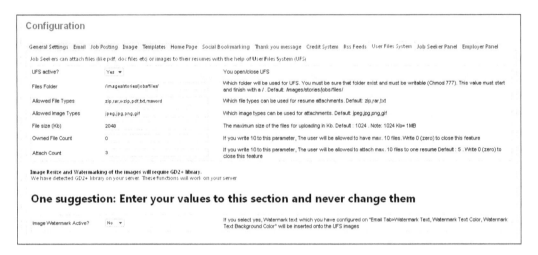

Job Seeker Panel

This tab provides the facility to change some jobseeker-related settings:

- **Resume Count**: You can limit here the number of resumes a job seeker can submit. Type the value **0** to offer unlimited resume submission.

- **Prevent Deleting of the last resume?**: This feature will prevent the user from deleting his/her last resume. The recommended setting is **Yes**.

- **Allow File Upload On Resume Creation**: Select the value **Yes** if you want to provide the facility to jobseekers to upload any external resume files during resume creation.

- **Job Alerts Active?**: You can activate this service to send jobseekers job alert services if they want to receive job alerts.

- **Job Alert Count**: You can enter any numeric values. The default value is **5**. It determines job alerts that will be sent for how many jobs.

Configuration

General Settings Email Job Posting Image Templates Home Page Social Bookmarking Thank you message Job Apply Page Credit System Rss Feeds User Files System

Job Seeker Panel | Employer Panel

Resume Count	5	How many resumes are job seekers allowed to have? For example: If you write 5 for this parameter, A job seeker can create a maximum of 5 resumes from their worker panel. Write 0 (zero) to close this parameter. 0 (zero) means that a job seeker can create unlimited resumes from the worker panel. Default : 5
Prevent Deleting of the last resume?	Yes ▼	If you select yes, Jobs! will prevent the job seeker from deleting the last resume the user has. SUGGESTED SETTING IS YES FOR THIS PARAMETER
Allow File Upload On Resume Creation	Yes ▼	http://www.instantphp.com/support/25-feature-request/6540-upload-resume-file-to-resume-files-tab.html

Job Alerts

Job Alerts Active?	Yes ▼	http://www.instantphp.com/doc
Job Alert Count	5	
Email Processing Type	Hosting panel cron jobs ▼	
Job Alert Count to process per cycle	500	

- **Email Processing Type:** This parameter defines the process of sending job alert e-mail. The default selection is **Hosting panel cron jobs.** Leave it as default.

- **Job Alert Count to process per cycle**: Define how many job alerts will be sent at a time. For example, if you enter the value **500**, then 500 alert mails will be sent at a time.

- **Job Count in Alert**: You can enter any numeric values. The default value is **5**. It defines how many jobs will be displayed in the job alert mail.

- **Job Alert Mail Subject**: Write the subject for the job alert mail. By default, a subject is provided, and you can change it as you want.

- **Job Alert Mail (HTML)**: By default, a sample e-mail is provided, and you can change it as you want from this editor area. This feature will send job alerts in HTML format and jobseekers will get the alerts in this format if they want to receive them in this format.

- **Job Alert Mail (Plain)**: Here also a sample e-mail is provided. You can change it easily from this editor area. This job alert e-mail will be sent as plain text e-mail. The jobseeker will get this mail in plain text format if they want to receive it in this format.

Employer Panel

This tab controls employer-related settings, such as:

- **Force Employers?**: If the selected option is **Yes**, they are forced to wait for your approval of their company.

- **Submission Confirm E-mail?**: When the selected option is **Yes**, after successful submission of company, the client will get a confirmation e-mail. This e-mail informs the employer that his/her company is successfully submitted for approval.

- **Inform Employer?**: The employer will get an e-mail after his/her submitted company's approval. The selected option must be **Yes** to get this notification. This e-mail confirms to the employer that his/her submitted company is approved.

- **Approve All New Companies?**: When the selected option is **Yes**, any new companies added by clients need your approval. To disable this feature, select the option **No**.

- **Message**: Write a message here that will be displayed in the employer panel of a client when the **Force Employers?** feature is active and no company of his/hers has been approved.

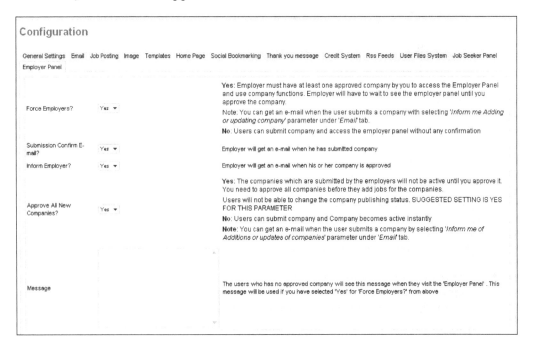

- **Company Count**: You can limit the number of companies allowed to be added by a client. The default value is **1**.

- **Inform employer on application?**: If you select the option **Yes**, the **Inform me?** feature will be offered for use to your clients. This feature enables your clients to get notification e-mails when a jobseeker applies for jobs.

Summary

The Global Configuration plays an important role in Joomla! 1.5 website development. Jobs! Pro Configuration setting is also another important tool to manage your jobsite. Both tools involve some complex settings. But this chapter provides a step-by-step guideline to configuring your jobsite and will help to resolve complexities.

5
Managing Jobs, Job Types, and Categories

In this chapter, we will learn about how to view and manage jobs, job types, and categories using the administrator control panel. Before adding a new job or managing jobs in your jobsite, you must add at least one job type and one category if there is no existence of a relevant job type or category, by default.

This chapter includes:

- Managing job types: View List Job Types, Add New Job Type, Edit Job Type, Publish Job Type, Unpublish Job Type, and Delete Job Type
- Managing job categories: View Jobs Category, Add new Category, Edit Category, Publish Category, Unpublish Category, and Delete Category
- Managing jobs: View List Jobs, Add new Job, Edit Jobs, Publish Jobs, Unpublish Jobs, and Delete Jobs

Introduction

Jobs! Pro 1.3.2 provides the facility to view and manage jobs, job types, and categories, with an easy user interface. Job types define the types of available jobs, such as temporary, part-time, full-time, internship, and others. On the other hand, job categories are used to classify jobs by their relevance, such as finance jobs, marketing jobs, technology jobs, and others. When your client posts a job for the position of *Marketing Executive*, it should be placed in the corresponding category *Marketing Jobs*.

Managing job types

A job type defines the job schedule or the kinds of job positions, such as part-time, full-time, internship, and others. Job types help jobseekers to find the most suitable job position, according to their aspirations. For example, a student may want to get a part-time job or an internship job only. You can manage job types only from the admin control panel. Job types help jobseekers to know about the availability of a job position, whether he or she is looking for these types of job or not.

Viewing List Job Types

To view the list of job types, first log into Joomla! 1.5 admin panel and then go to the Jobs! Pro 1.3.2 control panel.

Now click on the button **List Job Types** and this button opens the relevant window **List Job Types**. In this window, you will see the job types list. By default, the list contains some job type names, such as **Temporary**, **Student**, **Intern**, **Contract**, **Full Time**, **Part Time**, and others.

Adding a new job type

Job type helps jobseekers to get the right types of jobs, which are fit for their qualifications and the time available for working. If you want to add a new job type, click on the **Add New Job Type** tool in the **List Job Types** window. This tool opens the **Add New Job Type** window.

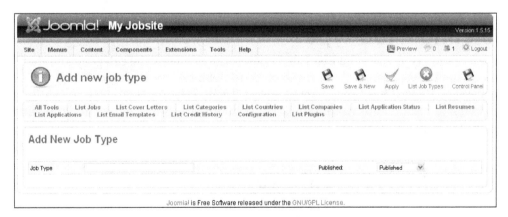

Now, provide the name in the **Job Type** field of this window and define the publishing status as **Published** or **Unpublished**. After this, click on the **Save** button to save the new job type.

Editing a job type

To edit any job type, select the job type by checking it from the **List Job types** window and then click on the **Edit** tool of this window.

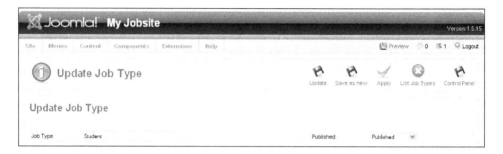

When the **Update Job Type** window opens, you can change the name, and after changing the name, click on the **Update** button to save the changes you made, or you can click on the **Save as New** button to save it as a new category.

Publishing or unpublishing a job type

To publish or unpublish a job type from the **List Job Types** window, check the job type and then click on either **Publish** or **Unpublish**. You will see the message **Record has been updated successfully**. Publishing or unpublishing a job type that is used in another process may affect the jobs that had been defined under this job type and may cause incorrect job listings. So, do not unpublish the job type that contains active records.

Deleting a job type

To delete a job type from the **List Job Types** window, check the category and then click on the **Delete** button. After the successful deletion of the category, you will see the message **Record has been deleted successfully**. Deleting a job type may affect jobs that had been defined under the job type that you want to delete. So, you will not be able to delete some job types.

Managing job categories

However, you can manage jobs categories in the administrator panel. But how many categories and which types of categories you intend to create depends on your objective. If you want to make a jobsite for medical professionals, it must contain categories that are related to the medical profession, such as physical therapist, occupational therapist, family practice physician, nursing, and others.

Viewing job categories

To view the list of job categories from Jobs! Pro 1.3.2 control panel, click on **List Categories**. When the **List Categories** window will be displayed, you will see a list of job categories by default, as shown in the following screenshot:

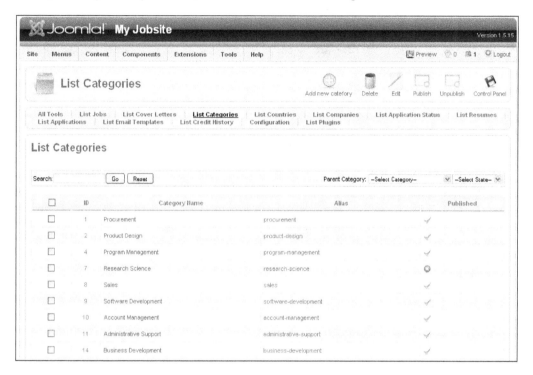

You can easily add a new category, delete, publish or unpublish, and edit any existing category from this window.

Adding a new category

In the **List Categories** window, click on the **Add new category** tool to add a new category. This tool opens the **Add new category** window.

You need to provide some basic information in the new window, such as:

- **Category Name**: Write the name of the category you want to create, for example, finance jobs, or marketing jobs.
- **Published**: Select a status from **Published** or **Unpublished**.

- **Alias**: It will be used to create search engine-friendly URLs. See *Chapter 4* for more information on using search engine-friendly URLs. You can leave this field blank to fill this up automatically.

- WYSIWYG editor: In this interface, you can write a description of your category.

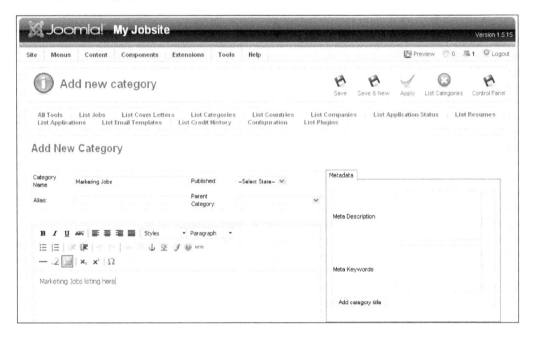

- **Meta Description**: You can add a short description in this field. It is not too necessary, so you can skip this.

- **Meta Keywords**: You can enter the keywords in this field in the **Metadata** section on the right-hand side. But it is better to skip this.

After providing your information, click on the **Save** button.

Editing a category

To edit a category, select the category by checking it from the **List Categories** window, and then click on the **Edit** tool in this window.

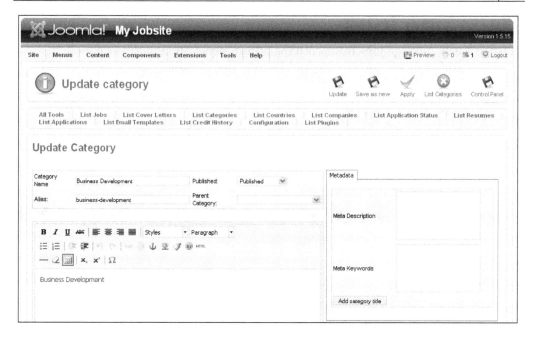

When the **Update Category** window opens, you can change any information that you want to update. After changing the information, click on the **Update** button of this window to save the changes you made or you can click on the **Save as New** button to save it as a new category.

Publishing or unpublishing a category

To publish or unpublish a category from the **List Categories** window, put a checkmark on the category and then click on the **Publish** button or **Unpublish** button. After this, you will see the message **Record has been updated successfully**. Publishing or unpublishing a category may affect jobs that had been classified under this category and may cause incorrect job listings. So do not unpublish any category that contains active records.

Deleting a category

To delete a category from the **List Categories** window, check the category and then click on the **Delete** button. After the successful deletion of the category, you will see the message **Record has been deleted successfully**. You will not able to delete some categories because of active records.

Managing jobs

You can easily manage jobs from both the admin panel and employer panel, including adding, viewing, editing, publishing, unpublishing, and deleting a job.

Viewing list jobs

To view the list of jobs from Jobs! Pro 1.3.2 control panel, click on the button **List Jobs**. This opens the window **List Jobs** with an empty list, as shown in the following screenshot:

Adding a new job

To add a new job from the **List Jobs** window, click on the **Add new Job** tool of this window. This tool is related to the **Add new job** window.

When the window opens, you may need to provide some mandatory information, such as:

- **Job**: Enter a job title (or the name of the job position) in this field, for example, senior executive, sales manager, and so on.
- **Published**: Select a status from **Published**, **Unpublished**, or **Draft**.

- **Category Name**: Select a category to which the new job belongs.

- **Job Description**: Write a full description of your job here. By default, this also has a WYSIWYG editor interface. You can use this editor to write your job description.

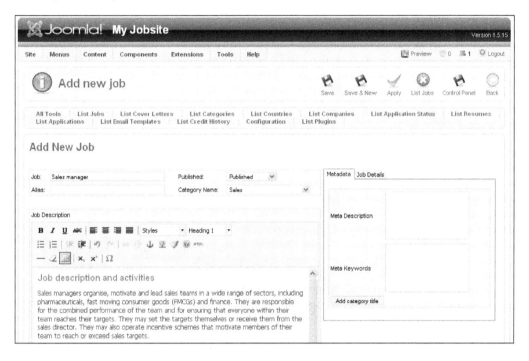

- **Job Qualification**: You can describe the required job qualification and other requirements for candidates in this editing area. It has also the same editor interface.

  You can provide also meta information, under the **Metadata** tab on the right-hand side. Meta information helps you to find jobs easily on search engine results.

- **Meta Description**: Type a short description here, which will be used as meta description of the job display page.

- **Meta Keywords**: Type some keywords in this field, or you can click on the **Add category title** button to add the job title as a keyword automatically. These keywords may be useful to find this job on search engines.

Now provide detailed information under the **Job Details** tab, which contains:

- **Company**: Select the company name from the list. If you are posting your own job, select your company. The company must be added before adding a job. See more information in the next chapter on how to add a new company.

- **Reference Number**: You can write a requisition number for this job. This number will be used on the job display page. This can be a number or a string, for example, *Ref: J12100*.

- **Number of Jobs**: In this field, enter the total number of job position(s).

- **Job Type**: Select a job type, such as part-time, full-time, or temporary.

- **Job Country**: **Select a country from the** drop-down list. If **Configuration | General Settings Tab | Make Jobs National** parameter is not zero, this feature will not show.

- **Job City**: Enter at least one city in this field. You can add multiple cities by separating each city with a comma.

- **Job State**: Enter at least one state in this field. You can also add multiple states by separating each state with a comma. This field is not a mandatory field because states are not common in all countries.

- **Experience (year)**: Enter a numerical value here to define the minimum level of experience for the job.

- **Preferred Degree**: Enter the level of preferred degree.

- **Yearly Job Salary ($)**: Enter the amount of salary (on per year basis).

- **Show Salary?**: You can define here whether salary will be shown or not. Selecting option **Yes** will show the salary and **No** will hide it.

- **Start Publishing**: Here, define the date of publishing the job announcement.

- **Stop Publishing**: Here, define the date to stop publishing. This job will be unpublished from this date.

- **Hits**: Shows hits counted for the job. You can not change this field's value.

- **Inform me**: Select **Yes** to get an e-mail notification when someone applies for this job. If **Configuration | Employer Panel | Inform employer on application?** parameter value is not **Yes**, this feature will not show.

Now click on **Save** at the top of the window. The new job will be saved and added to the jobsite.

Editing jobs

To edit a job from the **List Jobs** window of the admin control panel, select the job and then click on the **Edit Jobs** button (or you can directly click on the job). The **Update Job** window will be displayed.

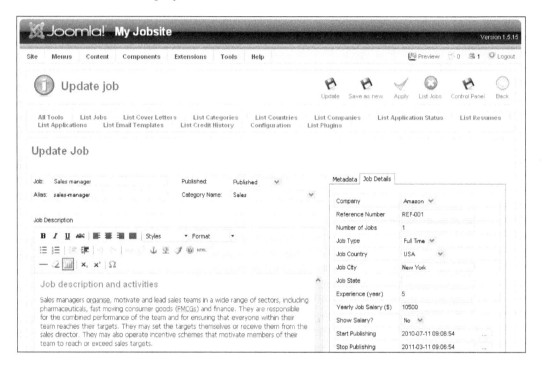

In this **Update Job** window, you can make any changes to your job as you need and then click on the **Save** button to save changes.

Publishing or unpublishing jobs

To publish or unpublish a job from the **List Jobs** window of the admin control panel, select the job and click on either **Publish** or **Unpublish**. If this succeeds, you will see the message **Record has been updated successfully**.

Deleting jobs

To delete a job from the **List Jobs** window, select the job and click on the **Delete** button. If this succeeds, you will see the message **Record has been deleted successfully**.

Summary

This chapter is written for a completely practical approach. After completing this chapter, you will have learned how to add, view, and manage jobs, job types, and categories using the Jobs! Pro 1.3.2 control panel. In the next chapter, you will learn how to manage employers' countries and companies in the Jobs! control panel.

6
Managing Countries and Companies

You can view and manage the list of countries from your Jobs! Pro administrator control panel. This list will be used in the **Company Details** section while adding a new company, and this is important to identify the country of a company. Administrator panel also lets you add and manage companies.

In this chapter, you will learn about:

- Managing countries
- Managing companies

Introduction

Before adding a company, you must ensure that the company country is listed in your website. For example, if you want to add a company from Bangladesh, you will not find the name **Bangladesh** in the company country list. So, before adding the company's information about a specific country, you need to add the country's name, in the list of countries.

Managing countries

You can easily view, add new country, and manage the names of the countries from the Jobs! Pro admin panel. By default, a few countries, such as USA, England, France, Germany, and others, are available on the list.

Viewing List Countries

In order to view the list of company countries from Joomla! 1.5 admin panel, click on the menu **Components** and then on **Jobs | List Countries**, as shown in the following screenshot:

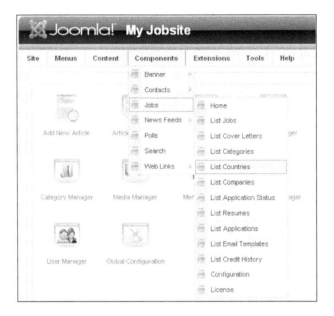

The **List Company Countries** window opens, as shown in the next screenshot. You can also access this window by clicking on the **List Countries** button in the Jobs! Pro admin control panel. The new window provides a list of predefined countries of the companies, such as USA, England, France, and others.

In this window, you can easily add a new country, or edit, delete, publish, or unpublish any country from the existing country list.

Adding new country

To add a new country in the **List Company Countries** window, click on the **Add new country** tool. This tool is related to the **Add new country** window (shown in the following screenshot):

Now provide a country name in the **Company Country** field. To omit any duplication, you must ensure that the country's name does not exist in the list already. After this, select the option **Published** from the list and then click on **Save**.

Editing country

Check the country you want to edit from the window **List Company Countries**, and then click on the **Edit** tool of this window.

The **Update Company Country** window will open; you can change the name of a country and its publishing status from this window. Click on the **Update** button to save the changes or click on the **Save & New** button to save it as a different one. Be careful while changing the name of the country of a company, as it may affect the records of all the companies connected to it.

Publishing or unpublishing countries

To publish or unpublish a country from the **List Company Countries** window, check the country and then click on either **Publish** or **Unpublish**. If successfully done, you will see the message **Record has been updated successfully**.

Deleting countries

To delete a country from the **List Company Countries** window, check the country name and then click on the **Delete** button; if it is deleted successfully, you will see the message **Record has been deleted successfully**. You will not be able to delete any country that is used in companies and you will see a message **Record has not been deleted because of active records**.

Managing companies

You can easily manage companies from the admin panel, for example, viewing list companies, adding a new company, editing companies, publishing or unpublishing a company, and deleting a company. These functions are very important for the maintenance of your jobsite.

Viewing List Companies

In order to view the list companies from Joomla! 1.5 admin panel, click on the menu **Components** and then **Jobs | List Companies** submenu, as shown in the next screenshot:

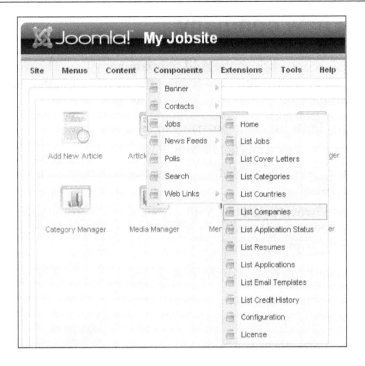

The window **List Companies** will open and you will see the list of companies in here. By default, this window may show a sample company **Amazon** in the list. See the following screenshot:

Adding a new company

To add a new company from the administrator control panel, go to the **List Companies** window and click on the **Add new company** tool. The window **Add new company** will open and you need to provide the relevant information in this window, for example:

- **Company**: Enter the company name in this field.

- **Alias**: You can leave this field blank. It will be useful for creating SEF URLs.

- **Published**: Select the publishing status, that is, whether published or unpublished.

- **Company Owner**: Select the employer's username from the drop-down list. You may see a capital letter E next to the username. The letter E defines it is a username of an employer.

You can write a short description of the new company in the WYSIWYG editor area.

You can also provide meta information under the **Metadata** tab on the right-hand side. But this information is not so important, so you can skip this step.

- **Meta Description**: Enter a short description here, which will be used as meta description

- **Meta Keywords**: Enter keywords in this field or click on the **Add category title** button to automatically add the company name as a keyword

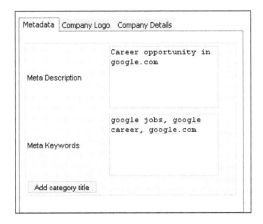

You can upload the company logo. To do this, click on the **Company Logo** tab, and select a logo by clicking on the **Browse** button. You are only allowed to upload JPEG, JPG, PNG, and GIF types of images, and file size should not be more than 1MB (1,024 KB). Refer to the next screenshot:

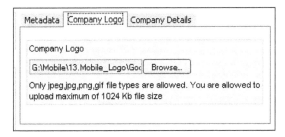

You will find the following parameters under the **Company Details** tab:

- **Address**: Enter the company address
- **Company Country**: Select the country of the company from the drop-down list
- **City**: Enter the company city
- **Zip**: Enter the company zip code
- **Company URL**: Enter the company URL, for example, http://www.google.com
- **Contact Name**: Enter the company contact name

- **Contact Email**: This is a mandatory field. Enter the company contact e-mail here

 Note: The contact e-mail is mandatory. You cannot leave this field blank. You must provide a valid e-mail address in this field. It will be used to contact the company or for sending notifications.

Now click on the **Save** button to save everything.

Editing a company

To edit a company from the admin panel, check the country you want to edit from the window **List Companies** and then click on the **Edit** tool of this window to open the **Update Company** window, as shown in the following screenshot:

When the **Update Company** window opens, change the required information and then click on the **Update** button to save the changes.

Publishing or unpublishing companies

To publish or unpublish a company from the admin panel, go to the **List Companies** window, check the company, and click on the **Publish** button or **Unpublish** button. You will see the confirmation message **Record has been updated successfully**.

Deleting companies

You can only delete a company from the admin panel. To delete a company from the admin panel, go to the **List Companies** window, check the company, and then click on the **Delete** button. After successful deletion, you will see the message **Record has been deleted successfully**. You can not delete any active records.

Summary

In this chapter, you have learned how to add a new country and how to manage list countries from the administrator control panel. You have also learned managing countries from both the admin and employer panel. This is important for the maintenance of your jobsite. In the next chapter, you will learn about managing e-mail, managing jobseekers' applications, and managing application status.

7
Managing E-mail, Applications, and Application Status

You can create e-mail templates that will help the employers to send responses to the applicants. You can also manage applications received from the candidates and the application status name.

This chapter includes:

- Managing e-mail templates
- Managing candidates' applications
- Managing application status

Introduction

E-mail template is a tool for employers and it will be shown to the employer and help the employer while responding to their candidates. Employers can create an e-mail template to accept or reject applications. It saves time and helps them respond to jobseekers faster. Also, you can easily manage e-mail templates and applications received from jobseekers. You can also manage the application status names. These names define whether an application is approved or rejected.

Managing e-mail templates

This feature is only for the employer and is known as an employer tool. E-mail templates help the employer to respond quickly to an applicant's application. The employer not only saves time, but also needs to make less effort to e-mail responses. You can easily manage all the e-mail templates added by you or by your employers from the administrator panel.

Viewing List Email Templates

You can easily view default and all of the saved e-mail templates. By viewing e-mail templates, you can see and control what e-mail templates are added frequently on your jobsite by your employers. In order to view the list of e-mail templates from the Jobs! Pro admin panel, click on **List Email Templates**.

You may see a list of the e-mail templates in the **List Email Templates** window. By default, it may contain only an empty list.

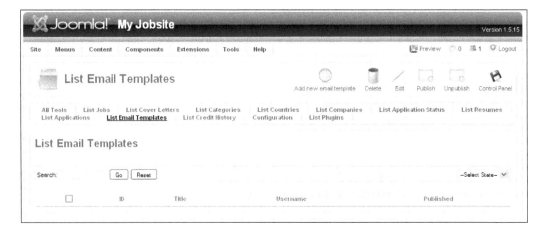

Adding a new e-mail template

Employers may need to use e-mail templates to respond to the applicants who applied for a job. It is the employers' task to add the e-mail templates from their control panel. But you can add the e-mail templates from the admin panel for any specific employer. To add a new e-mail template from the admin panel, click on **Add new email template**. Now you will see the **Add new email template** window. You need to provide the following information in this window:

- **Title**: Enter a title for your e-mail template in the field.

- **Username**: Select the user who can use this template. You will see J, B, or E, corresponding letters at the end of their usernames. J is a symbol for jobseeker; E is for employers, and B indicates blocked users. Here, select any employer username that contains the symbol E. For example: **demo_company-E**.

- **Published**: Select the publishing status, whether published or unpublished.

- **Email Template**: Write your message here. You can also use the following parameter in this message:

  `{COMPANY_NAME}`: Company name
  `{APPLICANT_NAME}`: Applicant Name
  `{JOB_TITLE}`: Job Title

  For example, you can write a message similar to the following:

  ```
  Dear {APPLICANT_NAME},
  Thank you so much! You are shortlisted for the job position: {
  JOB_TITLE}.
  Regards,
  Santonu Dhar
  {COMPANY_NAME}
  ```

Now, click on **Save** to save the new e-mail template, and when the template is saved, you will see the message **Record has been inserted successfully**.

Editing e-mail templates

If you need to make any corrections in an e-mail template or you need to make any changes such as changing template title or username, you need to edit the template.

To edit an e-mail template from **List Email Templates** window, you need to follow the next steps:

1. Select the template by putting a check mark on it and then click on **Edit**.

2. A relevant window will open; update the information that you want to change and click on **Update** in this window.

3. When all the information is successfully updated, you will see the message **Record has been updated successfully**.

Publishing or unpublishing an e-mail template

If you do not want to use an e-mail template, you can publish or unpublish. To publish or unpublish e-mail templates from the admin panel, select the e-mail template and then click on the **Publish** or the **Unpublish** button. The publishing status will be changed and you will see the message **Record has been deleted successfully**.

Deleting e-mail templates

If you do not need an e-mail template, you can delete it. To delete e-mail templates, select the e-mail template from the **List Email Templates** window, and click on **Delete**. When the template is deleted, you will see the message **Record has been updated successfully**.

Managing applications

You will be able to view and manage the applications to your jobs and the applicants' resumes. You will also be able to contact your applicant with the module.

Viewing List Applications

Applications are received from the candidates who have applied for jobs. To view the list of applications from Jobs! Pro admin panel, click on **List Applications**.

The window **List Applications** will be displayed. In this window, you will see the list of applications received from the candidates.

Editing applications

To edit applications from the admin panel, you must go to the **List Applications** window, then select an application by putting a check and click on **Edit**.

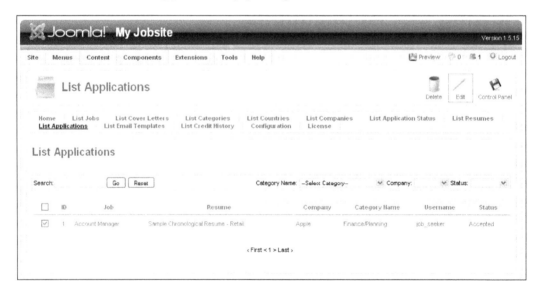

Now, the window **Update Application** will open. You will see following five tabs in this window — **Resume**, **Job Details**, **Application Details**, **Email History**, and **Application History**.

In the default tab **Resume**, you will see a cover letter and the applicant's resume.

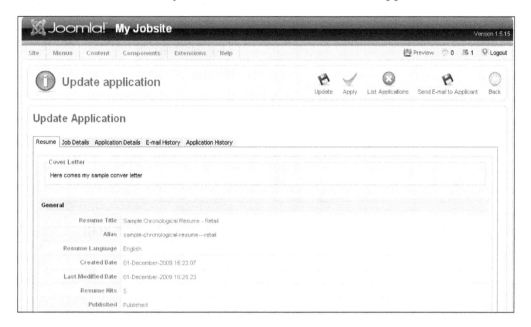

The next tab **Job Details** displays the details of your job. You cannot make any changes here.

In the **Application Details** tab, you will see the application **Status, Application Date, Last Modification Date**, and so on. You can change the status by clicking on the drop-down list next to **Status**. Default status values are **Accepted** and **Rejected**. You can also add comments in the **Application Comments** text area.

You will see the history of e-mail responses to the applicant in the **E-mail History** tab.

If you have not yet responded to the applicant and want to respond, select an e-mail template, depending on what type of message you want to send to the applicant. You can change the employer's default e-mail address on **Your E-mail** field; you can even change the applicant's (recipient's) e-mail address with the help of **Application E-mail** field. You can write a new subject for an e-mail or modify the default subject in the **E-mail Subject** field. You can also change the message you want to send to the applicants in the **E-mail Body** area.

Now click on **Send E-mail to Applicant** to send the message to the applicant. You will see the confirmation message when your e-mail is sent to applicant: for example, **Your e-mail has been sent to Paul Jones**.

You can also view the application received from this user for other jobs posted by the same company in the **Application History** tab.

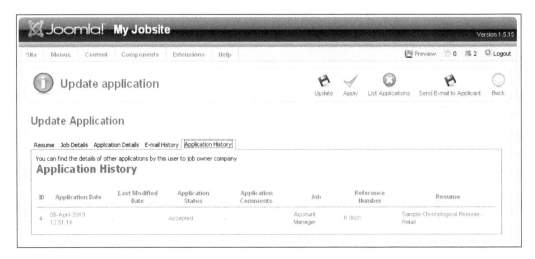

Now click on **Save** to save everything.

Deleting applications

To delete applications, go to admin panel and then go to the **List Applications** window, select the application by check marking it and then click on the **Delete** button. The application will be deleted.

Managing application status

Application status defines the status of an application whether it is accepted or rejected. You can manage application status only from the admin panel.

Viewing List Status

To view the list of application status from Jobs! Pro admin panel, click on **List Application Status**.

Now the **List Application Status** window opens, and here you can see the status of the applications.

Adding a new status name

To add a new status name from the admin panel, click on the **Add new status** button in the **List Application Status** window. Now you will see the window **Add new status.** You need to provide a status name and also need to define the publishing status in this window. See the next screenshot:

After that, click on **Save** or **Save & new** to add the new status.

Editing status name

To edit a status name from the admin panel, you first need to select the status name by putting a check on it and then click on **Edit** in the **List Status** menu.

In the new window, you will be able to change the name of application status and you can also define whether it will be published or not.

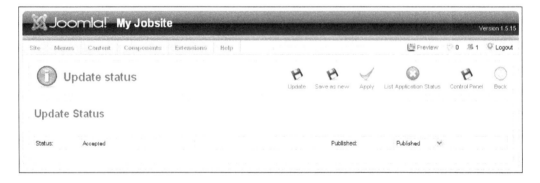

Now click on **Update** to save changes.

Publishing or unpublishing a status name

If you do not want to use an application status name, you can change its publishing status to **Unpublished**. In the same way, you can use any template by publishing it. To publish or unpublish an application status name from the **List Status** window, select the status name first and then click on the **Publish** or **Unpublish** button.

Deleting status name

If you no longer need a status name in your jobsite, you can delete the status name. To delete a status name from the admin panel, select the status name from the **List Status** window and then click on **Delete**.

Summary

This chapter provides guidelines to create an e-mail template that will be used to respond to the applicants. You have also learned how to manage applications and status. After reading this chapter, you will be able to manage your e-mail templates, applications, and application status easily.

8
User Registration, Credits, Resume Fields, and Education Levels

You can entirely control the user registration system from the Jobs! Pro admin panel and extend its power. We can even charge the users a certain amount of money for a specific service because Jobs! Pro has an exclusive feature credit system, which can be fully configured from the admin panel.

In this chapter, we will learn about:

- Adding a jobseeker and an employer
- Viewing the list of jobseekers
- Viewing the list of employers
- Managing the credit system
- Managing resume fields and categories
- Managing education levels

Introduction

Jobs! Pro can automatically detect whether a user is a jobseeker or an employer, based on what they have—a resume or a company. We can use a credit system in our jobsite. This system is used to control credits and users need to purchase enough credit for a particular task.

We can also change default resume fields and education levels in the Jobs! Pro control panel. Resume fields help to collect necessary information from the jobseekers to complete his/her resume. On the other hand, **Education Levels** is the shortest form for providing an educational qualification.

Adding a jobseeker and an employer

If we want to register as a jobseeker, we need to create a resume for the user. This resume will recognize the user as a jobseeker. On the other hand, if we want to add an employer account, we need to add a company.

In Jobs! Pro, you can add a jobseeker or an employer in two ways:

- Using no extra plugins
- With the help of plugins

Using no extra plugins

This is a simple and recommended method. The user first registers with a user management component such as default Joomla! registration system or any user management components, for example, Community Builder. When the user completes registration and visits the front page of Jobs! Pro, they will be forced to create a profile of an employer or a jobseeker.

In order to use this feature, you need to define the **On First Visit** option as **Profile Creation Method** parameter value in the **Configuration** window. To do this, go to the menu **Components | Jobs | Configuration**, and you will find the parameter in the **General Settings** tab.

| General Settings | Email | Job Posting | Image | Templates | Home Page | Social Bookmarking | Thank you message | Job Apply Page | Credit System | Rss Feeds | User Files System |

Job Seeker Panel   Employer Panel

Download ID	f087dda59f65758a2371!	You need to write your DownloadID to validate your installation. If you do not know your DownloadID, Please click here to edit your license details
Date Format	01-06-2007 14:35:12 ▾	Select the date format you want to use
Records on a page	20	Records on a page
Language	english ▾	Component language
Default Status	Accepted ▾	Status when a user applies for a job
Activate Company functions	Yes ▾	If you select 'Yes', Your users will be able to add their companies (and using related function like job posting, responding to the applicants, searching the resume database) to your web site. This is an ideal solution , if you are using com_jobs for only your company (only one company) If you are using our component to run a career portal like monster.com, Select 'Yes' for this option. Note: 'Super Administrator' user group is out of this criteria
Activate Job Seeker Functions	Yes ▾	If you select 'Yes', Your users will be able to add their resumes (and using related job seeker functions like job cover letters, making applications to the jobs) to your web site. Note: 'Super Administrator' user group is out of this criteria
Show Toolbar?	Show ▾	You can show or hide the component toolbar. Suggested setting is Show.
Category Order	Title Descending ▾	Select the order for job categories
Make Jobs! National	0	Country Field is used for company details and Job Details for Jobs! design. This parameter helps you to **hide** the country field for your employers and job seekers. Country Fied will continue to exist but any of your visitors/employers/job seeker will see it. You will continue to see the country fields on admin panel * Write country id you want to use. Visit *Joomla Admin Panel>Components>Jobs>List Countries* . Add new country and write the id of your country. Make sure that country is published * write 0 (zero) to close this feature
Hide Company?	Show All Company Details ▾	* Show All Company Details: Jobs! will show company details to the job seekers and public * Allow Company Choose: A "Hide Company Name?" option will appear on job form. This will be an option employers to be able to post jobs anonymously. * Hide All Company Details: This will hide "Company Details" from job seekers and public. Job Seeker will be able to see company details after he makes an application to the job
Profile Creation Method	On First Visit ▾	* On First Visit: Jobs! will force your users to create their employer or job seeker profile on first visit to Jobs! . See this screenshot to have better idea. WE SUGEGST YOU TO SELECT THIS OPTION FOR THIS PARAMETER * With Plugins: You need to install the seperate registration related plugins which are provided with Jobs! package

If you want to use the first method (with the help of plugins), select the option
With Plugins.

With the help of plugins

This is a complex method and is not recommended. Jobs! Pro has two plugins for
user registration. Both plugins are Joomla! user plugins (by default, Joomla! has
authentication, content, editors, editors-xtd, search, system, user, xmlrpc plugin
types, and so on).

- **lkncbjobsregister** plugin: This plugin will work with Community Builder.
  This plugin helps to register the user as an employer or a jobseeker.

- **lknjoomlajobsregister**: This plugin can work with the other user
  management components. This plugin can create only a jobseeker.

If you are going to use the lkncbjobsregister plugin to create a system for employer registration, first you need to create some extra fields in the Community Builder Custom field manager for the company data. **Community Builder** (**CB**) is a popular Joomla! component and it extends the Joomla! user management system. If you have not installed it yet, go to its official site `http://www.joomlapolis.com/` and download the latest version of Community Builder. It is a non-commercial extension and available on GPLv2 license. Main key features of this extension are extra fields in profile, enhanced registration workflows, user lists, connection paths between users, admin-defined tabs and user profiles, image upload, frontend workflow management, and integration with other components, such as PMS, newsletter, forums, and galleries.

After downloading Community Builder extension, go to the Joomla! admin panel and click on menu **Extensions | Install/Uninstall** to open installer window. Now select `com_comprofiler.zip` file from the installer package and install this like other extensions. After successful installation, you will see the following screen:

The idea behind the development of this plugin is as follows:

- If the user enters company data, make him/her the employer
- If the user does not enter company data, make him/her the jobseeker

There are two steps for using this plugin:

- Creating fields for this plugin
- Installing and configuring the plugin

To create the fields section for Community Builder, go to Joomla! admin panel and select the menu **Components | Community Builder | Field Management**.

The relevant window will open. Now click on the **New Field** button in this window and then create four custom fields one by one, as shown in the next table:

Name	Title	Field Type	Required	Published
cb_jobscompanytitle	Company Title	Textbox	No	Yes
cb_jobscompanycompanyurl	Company Url	Textbox	No	Yes
cb_jobscompanyaddress	Company Address	Textarea	No	Yes
cb_jobscompanydescription	Company Description	Textarea	No	Yes

After creation of these fields, open the **CB Field Manager** window. Here, you will see these fields in a list as shown in the next screenshot:

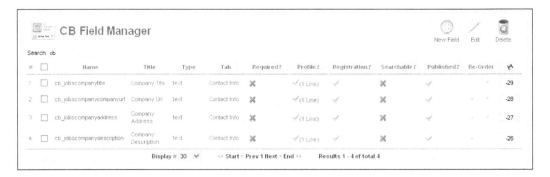

Next, you need to install and configure the lkncbjobsregister plugin. You will get this plugin with your Jobs! Pro bundle. Install it from the installer window. To go to the installer window click on menu **Extension | Install/Uninstall** from Joomla! admin panel. Now, install it using one of the three options for installation — **Upload Package File**, **Install from Directory**, or **Install from URL**. After this, configure the plugin by changing some parameters in the **Plugin Manager** window, such as the following:

- **Default Country ID**: When the user submits a new company during the registration process, a country will be used by default. You can define the default country by providing a country ID here. The country ID must be valid. You will find the country ID in the **List Countries** window. To go to this window, click on the **Components** menu and then select **Jobs | List Countries** submenu from Joomla! 1.5 admin panel. You will see all the IDs in the first column of the company countries list of the **List Countries** window.

- **Default Resume Title**: Enter a title for the default resume.

- **Default Resume Status**: Define the default resume status, whether it is enabled or disabled. By default it is disabled.

- **Default Resume Language**: Enter a language in this field. By default, the language is **English**.

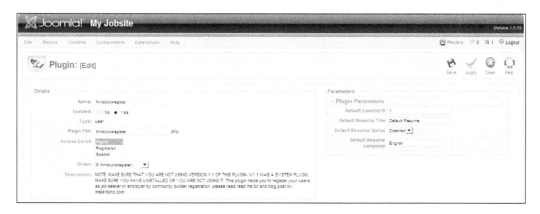

Next, you will be able to register any employer with the help of the Community Builder (CB) component.

Viewing List Job Seekers

Let's have a look at the list of jobseekers:

1. Click on the menu **Components| Jobs | Home** and go to the Jobs! 1.2 control panel. Click on **List Job Seekers**.

2. In this window, you will see all the registered jobseekers.

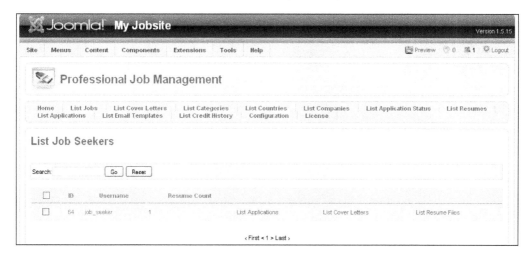

3. In this window, we will be able to view and manage their applications, cover letters, and resume files by clicking on the corresponding links.

Viewing List Employers

Now let's have a look at the list of employers:

1. Click on **List Jobseekers** from Jobs! Pro control panel.

2. The window **List Employers** will appear. You will see all the registered employers in this window.

3. In this window, we will be able to view and manage their jobs and e-mail templates by clicking on the corresponding links.

Managing the credit system

Credit system is a system allowing people to purchase products or services on credit. We can use this credit system in our jobsite to enforce clients, especially employers, to purchase credits. No employer will be able to use specific services (such as job posting, resume search, and so on) until they pay for purchasing new credit. This means that we can limit services and charge clients for extra credits they want to purchase (for details, see *Chapter 4*).

We can manage credits from the **Credit System** section of Jobs! Pro control panel. There are two buttons in this section—**List Credit History** and **List Pending Credits**.

The **List Credit History** feature will help you to view or edit credits and also to add new credits. The **List Pending Credits** feature will help you to view pending credits, and you will be able to approve or reject any pending credits.

Viewing or editing credits

If you want to view the total credits of the employers, click on **List Credit History**. The relevant window will open and you will see the total credits.

To change the number of credits and view the credit history for a specific employer (such as credit buying history and credit spending history), click on the employer name link or put a checkmark on the employer from the list in this window. After this, click on **Edit/View**. A new window will appear and you will see the total credits of this user. For example, if the total credits are five, this means that currently the employer has totally five credits. The employer will not be able to post a job or complete any other task exceeding the credit limit. You can also limit the resume searching facility for a certain time. The employer will not be able to search resumes after the date expires.

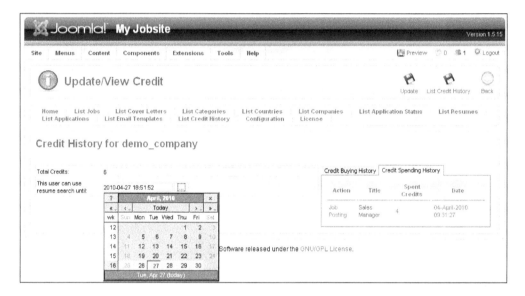

This window contains two tabs—**Credit Buying History** and **Credit Spending History**—on the right side of the window. You will see all the credits the employer buys in the **Credit Buying History** tab, and you will also see how many credits are spent and for what in the **Credit Spending History** tab.

Adding new credit

To add new credit for employers, click on **Add New Credit** in the **List Credit History** window. Now fill up all the fields with necessary information, such as the following:

- **Username drop-down list:** You need to specify first that you are adding credit for a specific employer. Select the username of the employer from the drop-down list. You will see a letter E with the employer's username. This helps you to identify an employer.

- **Payer Email field**: This field is optional. If you have received your payment through a merchant service such as PayPal, you can enter the payer's e-mail address in this field.

- **Currency field:** This field is optional. Enter the currency for the payment you received in this field.

- **Bought Credits field:** In this field, enter the number of credits bought by the employer.

- **Verify Sign field**: This field is optional. You can enter whether to verify and sign for the payment.

- **Transaction ID field:** This field is also optional. Enter the unique ID of payment in this field.

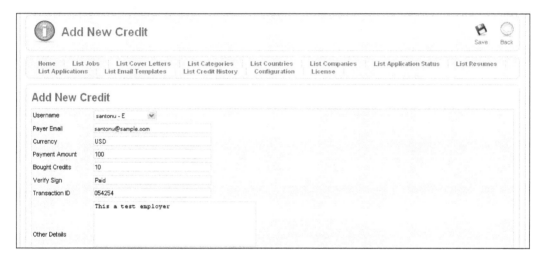

After providing all the information, click on the **Save** button and close the window.

Accepting or rejecting pending credits

When an employer buys credit from their employer panel, it will be pending for your approval. To view, approve, or reject the pending credits, click on **List Pending Credits** and when the relevant window opens, put a checkmark on the pending credit and click on **Approve/Reject** to respond. If you have no pending credits, you will see the message, **There are no pending credits**.

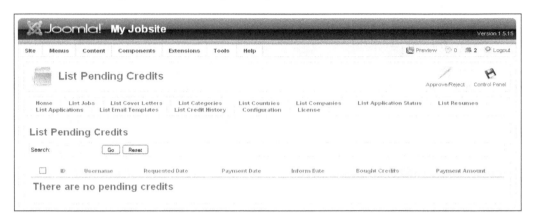

Managing resume fields and categories

Resume fields are used to collect information from jobseekers through resume submission form. We can manage all the resume fields and resume field categories from our Jobs! Pro 1.3.2 admin control panel.

Viewing List Resume Fields

For viewing list resume fields:

1. Click on **List Resume Fields**.

2. The window **List Resume Fields** will open and you will see a list of resume fields.

Adding a new resume field

To add a new field, click on **New Field** in the **List Resume Fields** window. The window **Add Resume Field** will be displayed. You need to input some related information in this window such as the following:

- **Type**: Select the type of field, for example, **Text Area**.
- **Field Name**: Enter a name for the new field. The prefix "lknjobs_" will be automatically added to the name. For example, if you enter the name **email**, it will be automatically changed to **lknjobs_email**.
- **Field Category**: Select the category of the resume field that it belongs to. For example, the Email field should be in the category **Personal**.
- **Title**: Enter a title in this field, for example, **Email Address**.

- **Tooltip**: Enter a tooltip in this field. It will help the jobseekers to fill it.

- **Search Tooltip:** This tooltip will be shown in the resume search page.
- **Error Message**: Enter a message here. This message will be shown to the user in the JavaScript pop-up message window if the user does not enter the required value.
- **Required**: If this field is mandatory, select the value **Yes**.
- **Published**: Select the publishing status, whether it is published or not.
- **Searchable**: If you select **Yes**, this field will be searchable from the resume search section. If you do not want to show the field in the resume search section, select the value **No** for this field.
- **Size**: Define the size here in numeric value, for example, 20, 25, and so on.
- **Max Length**: Define the maximum length in numeric value. By default, it is 20.

After providing all the information, click on **Save** or **Save & New**.

Editing a resume field

To edit a resume field, follow these steps:

1. Go to the **List Resume Fields** window, select the resume field and then click on **Edit**.

2. The **Update Resume Field** window will open. Now make the required changes in this window.

3. After making the changes, click on **Update** to save the changes.

Publishing or unpublishing a resume field

In order to publish or unpublish a resume field, first go to the **List Resume Fields** window and select the resume field and then click on **Publish** or **Unpublish.** When the resume field is published or unpublished successfully, you will see the message, **Record has been updated successfully**.

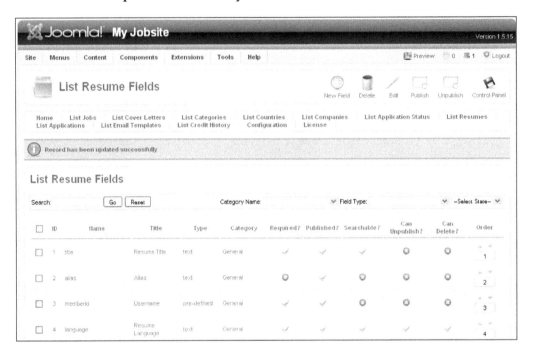

Deleting a resume field

If you want to delete a resume field, first go to the **List Resume Fields** window and select the resume field and then click on **Delete**. When the resume field is deleted successfully, you will see a message, **Field with 187 is deleted**.

Viewing List Resume Field Categories

To view the list of resume fields categories, click on **List Resume Field Categories** from Jobs! admin control panel.

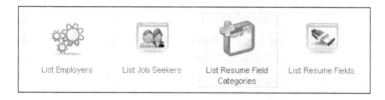

The window **List Resume Field Categories** opens and you will see a list of resume field categories in the window.

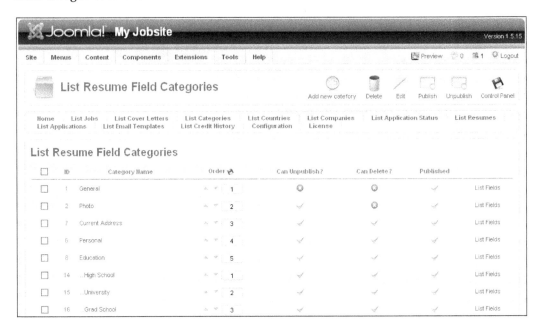

Adding a new resume field category

In order to add a new resume field category, click on **Add New Category** in the window **List Resume Field Categories**. The window **Add New Resume Field Category** will appear. You need to provide some related information in this window:

- **Category Name**: Enter a name for the new category, for example, Personal Information.

- **Parent Category**: To place a new category under an existing category, select the existing category as a parent category from the drop-down list. If you do not select a category, it will be in root position.

- **Published**: Define whether it will be published or remain unpublished.

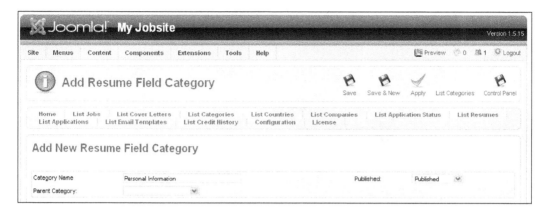

After providing the information, click on **Save** or **Save & New** to add the new category.

Editing resume field categories

To edit a resume field category:

1. Go to the **List Resume Fields Categories** window and select a category and then click on the **Edit** button.

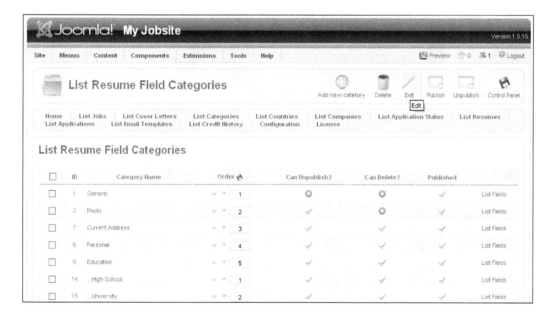

2. The **Update Resume Field Category** window will open; now edit any information in this window.

3. After changing the information, click on **Update** or **Save as new** to save the changes.

Publishing or unpublishing resume field categories

In order to publish or unpublish a field category, first select the resume field and then click on the **Publish** or **Unpublish** button in the **List Resume Field Categories** window. When the resume field category is published or unpublished successfully, you will see a message, **Record has been updated successfully**.

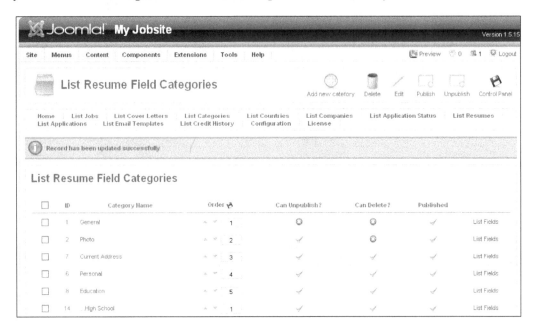

Deleting a resume field category

To delete a resume field category, go to the **List Resume Field Categories** window and select the field category and then click on **Delete**. When the resume field category is deleted successfully, you will see a message **Record has been deleted successfully**.

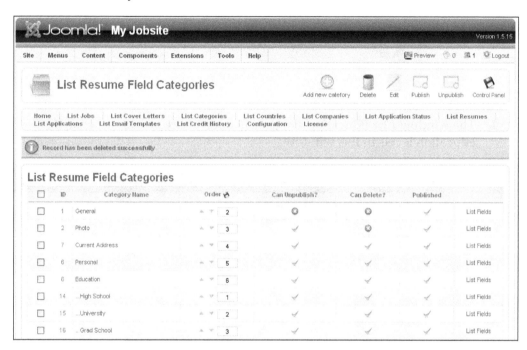

Managing education levels

Education levels are used in the jobseekers' resume submission form to show levels of educational qualification of the jobseekers. It saves time as the jobseeker need not write his/her education levels; they just need to select it from the drop-down list. You can add new educational levels and manage others from your Jobs! 1.2 control panel.

Viewing List Education Levels

To view list education levels:

1. First click on the button **List Education Levels** in the Jobs! 1.2 admin control panel.

2. The window **List Education Levels** will open and you will see a list of education levels in this window.

Adding a new education level

To add a new education level, click on the **Add New Education Level** button of the window **List Education Levels.** The window **Add New Education Level** will be shown. You need to provide the following information in this window:

- **Education Level**: Enter the level of education, for example, **High School Degree**.

- **Published**: Also, define whether it will be published or remain unpublished.

- After providing a name in the **Education Level** field and defining the publishing status, click on **Save** or **Save & New** to add the new education level.

Editing education levels

To edit an education level, follow the steps:

1. Go to the **List Education Levels** window and select the education level and then click on **Edit**.

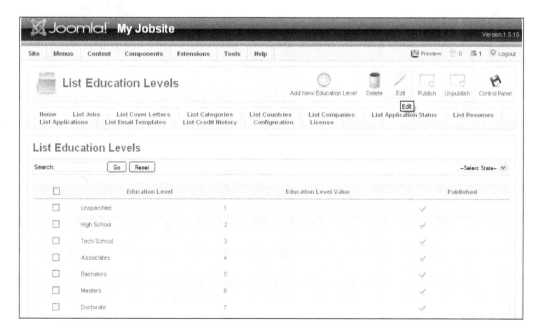

2. The **Update Education Level** window will open; now make the changes to this window.

3. After changing any information, click on the button **Update** or **Save as new** to save the changes.

Publishing or unpublishing education levels

To publish or unpublish education levels first select an education level and then click on the **Publish** or **Unpublish** button in the **List Education Levels** window. When the education level is published or unpublished successfully, you will see a message, **Record has been updated successfully**.

Deleting education levels

To delete any education level, go to the **List Education Levels** window and select the education level and then click on **Delete**. When the education level is deleted successfully, you will see a message, **Record has been deleted successfully**.

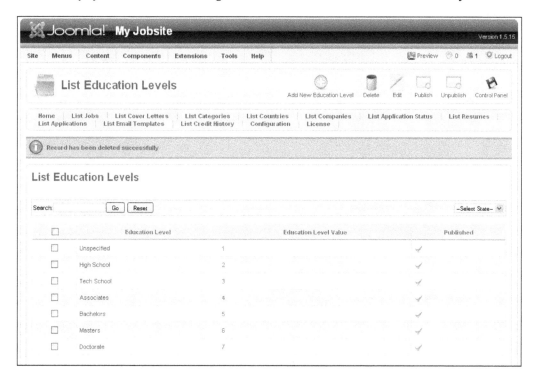

Summary

This chapter explained some complex and critical tasks such as the user registration system, managing employer credits, managing resume fields, and education levels. After completing this chapter, you will have learned how to register an employer or a jobseeker and how to manage credits. You will have also learned how to add or remove resume fields, resume field categories, and education levels. In the next chapter, you will learn how to manage cover letters, resumes, and resume files.

9
Managing Cover Letter, Resume, and Resume Files

Jobseekers can easily add a new cover letter, resume, and resume files from the frontend control panel, by using jobseeker tools. As the site administrator, we may need to manage these cover letters, resumes, and resume files. Cover letters and resumes are important when a candidate applies for a job. A jobseeker will not be able to apply for a job without creating his or her resume.

In this chapter, we will learn about:

- Managing cover letters
- Managing resumes
- Managing resume files

Introduction

When a jobseeker applies for a job, he/she needs to write a cover letter. A cover letter is usually used as an application and explains what the applicant has applied for. Employers will see this cover letter before viewing the resume. Therefore, a good cover letter helps to get an approval easily and also helps with being shortlisted for an interview.

A resume represents one's career, education, skills, and contact information. Jobseekers will be able to add more than one resume on the website. They can also add additional information by uploading external resume files. We can easily manage these cover letters, resumes, and resume files from the backend of the Jobs! admin panel.

Managing cover letters

You can manage cover letters both from the admin panel and jobseeker panel. The Jobs! Pro admin panel enables you to manage all the cover letters. But from the jobseeker panel, you can manage only cover letters of jobseekers who are logged in.

Viewing cover letters

Let's have a look at the cover letters.

First, go to Jobs! admin control panel and then click on **List Cover Letters**.

The relevant window will appear and you will see a list of cover letters in this window.

Adding a new cover letter

To add a new cover letter from the Jobs! Pro admin panel, first click on **Add cover letter** in the **List Cover Letters** window.

The **Add New Cover Letter** window opens. Now you need to provide the following information in this window:

- **Username**: First, you need to specify the jobseeker for whom you are adding the cover letter. Select the username of the jobseeker from the drop-down list. You will see a letter **J** with the jobseeker's username, which helps you to identify a jobseeker.

- **Title**: Enter a title for the cover letter in this field, for example, **My Cover Letter**.

- **Cover Letter**: Write the cover letter in this text area. We can also copy and paste a cover letter from Word or any other text editor.

- **Published**: Select the publishing status, whether it will be published or unpublished.

- After providing all the information, click on **Save** to save the new cover letter.

Updating a cover letter

To update the cover letter:

1. Click on **Edit** in the **List Cover Letters** window of Jobs! admin panel.

2. The relevant window **Update cover letter** opens and you can make the required changes in this window.

3. Click on **Update** to save the changes you made.

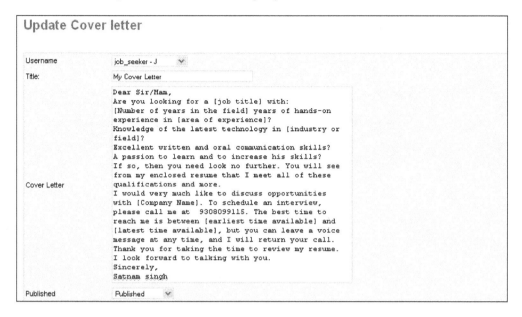

Publishing or unpublishing a cover letter

When a cover letter is unpublished, you will not be able to use it without changing its publishing status. On the other hand, if you do not want to use a cover letter, you can change its publishing status to unpublished.

In order to publish or unpublish a cover letter from the Jobs! Pro admin panel:

First, select the cover letter from the **List Cover Letters** window and then click on **Publish** or **Unpublish**.

You will see the message, **Record has been updated successfully**, when the publishing status is changed.

Deleting a cover letter

To delete a cover letter from the Jobs! Pro admin panel:

First, select the cover letter in the List Cover Letters window and then click on **Delete**.

You will see the message, **Record has been deleted successfully**, when the cover letter is deleted.

Managing resumes

You can also manage resumes from both the Jobs! admin panel and jobseeker panel. The jobseeker panel allows managing resumes of only those jobseekers who are currently logged in.

Viewing List Resumes

To view the list of resumes from Jobs! Pro admin panel:

1. First, click on the **List Resumes**.

2.   The **List Resumes** window opens and you will see a list of resumes.

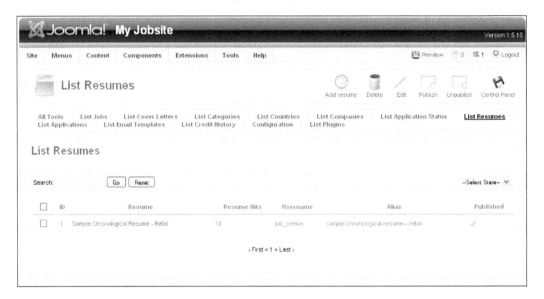

Adding a new resume

To add a new resume from Jobs! Pro admin panel:

1.   Click on **Add resume** of the **List Resumes** window.

2. The **Add new resume** window will open. By default, this window contains 13 tabs—**General**, **Photo**, **Current Address**, **Personal**, **Education**, **Languages**, **Employment**, **Recent Employers**, **Job skills**, **References**, **Text Resume**, **Banned Companies**, and **Resume Files**.

In this window, you need to provide some mandatory and basic information in the **General** tab, as follows:

- ◦ **Resume Title**: Enter a title for the resume here, for example, **My Resume**.

- ◦ **Username**: You first need to specify the jobseeker for whom you are adding a cover letter. Select the username of the jobseeker from the drop-down list. You will see a letter **J** with the jobseeker's username. This helps you to identify a jobseeker.

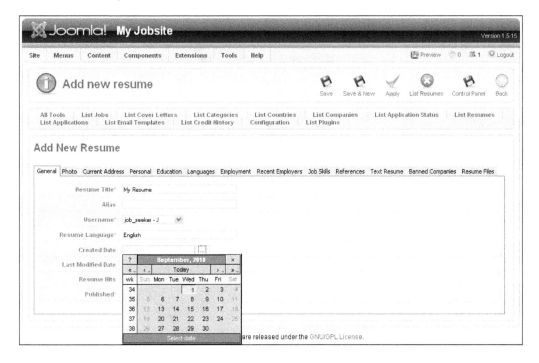

- ◦ **Resume Language**: You must enter the language of the resume. Enter the name of a language this should be written in title case, for example, **English**.

- ◦ **Created Date**: Enter the creation date of the resume.

- ◦ **Published**: Select the publishing status, whether the resume will be published or unpublished.

⚬ You can upload an image for your resume in the **Photo** tab.
Click on **Browse** and select an image from your computer.

⚬ In the **Current Address** tab, provide the details of your
present address by filling up fields, such as **Street**, **City**,
State, **Zip Code**, and others.

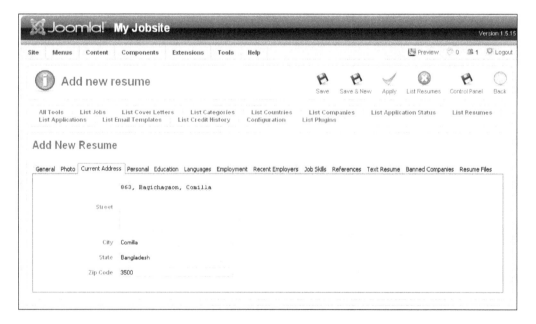

- In the next tab—**Personal**—you need to provide some personal information, such as **Full Name**, **Home Phone**, **Work Phone**, **Cell Phone**, **Email Address**, and so on. Here there is also an option **I'm currently working**. Select the value **No** here if the jobseeker is not working anywhere currently.

- In the **Education** tab, you need to provide educational details, including **High School**, **University**, **Graduate School**, and others.

Add New Resume

General Photo Current Address Personal **Education** Languages Employment Recent Employers Job Skills References Text Resume Banned Companies Resume Files

High School

School	Zila School
City	Comilla
State	Bangladesh

University

School	University of Wales
City	Dhaka
State	Dhaka
Degree/Certification Diploma	BSC
Area of Study	Computer Science
Diploma	Graduate

- ° In the **Languages** tab, you need to provide information about the languages known. You have to select levels of language skills separately for **Reading**, **Writing**, and **Understanding**. By default, you can add information about four languages.

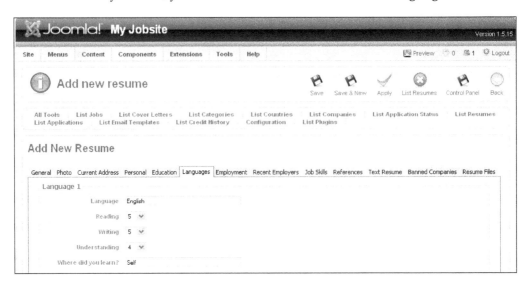

- ° The **Employment** tab enables you to add employment details, such as **Date You Can Start** to work, **Desired Yearly Salary**, **Job Type**, and so on.

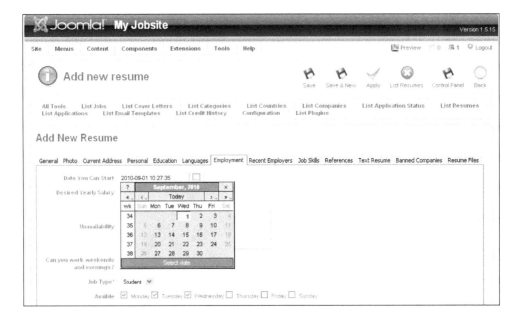

○ In the **Recent Employers** tab, you need to provide details of experience and employment history—**Total Experience**, **Most Recent Employer**, **Prior Employer**, and so on. If you are adding a fresh jobseeker's resume, you can leave this field blank.

○ The **Job Skills** tab helps you to provide information about any additional job skills, such as driving license or computer knowledge.

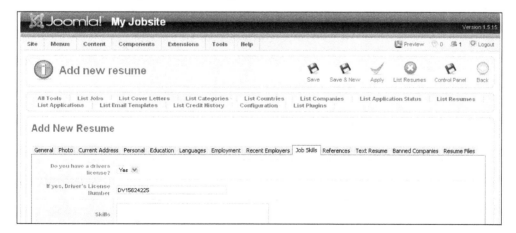

- The **Reference** tab allows you to add references. By default, you can add four references.

- The **Text Resume** tab provides a facility to write a text resume. You can also paste your resume here from a Word document.

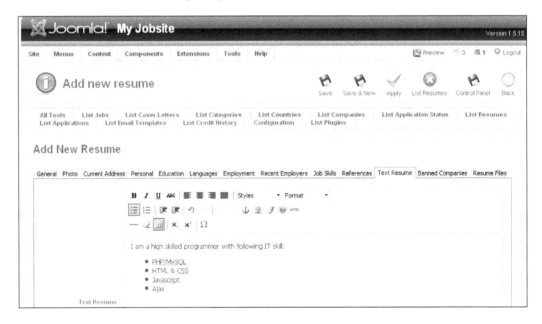

° In the **Banned Companies** tab, you can block certain companies from viewing your resume. The companies you select will not be able to view any part of your resume.

° The next tab, **Resume Files**, enables you to select the resume files you uploaded earlier.

° After providing all the information, click on the button **Save** to save the new resume.

Updating a resume

To edit or update a resume from Jobs! Pro admin panel:

1. Open the **List Resumes** window and click on **Edit** in the **List Resume Files** window.

2. The **Update resume** window will display. Change the required information in the tabs of this window. This window is similar to **Add new resume** window.

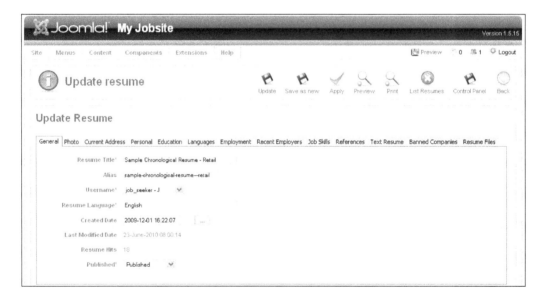

3. Click on **Update** to save the changes. You can also click on **Save as new** to add it as a new resume.

Publishing or unpublishing a resume

To publish or unpublish resumes from Jobs! Pro admin panel:

1. First, select the resume and then click on **Publish** or **Unpublish** in the **List Resumes** window.

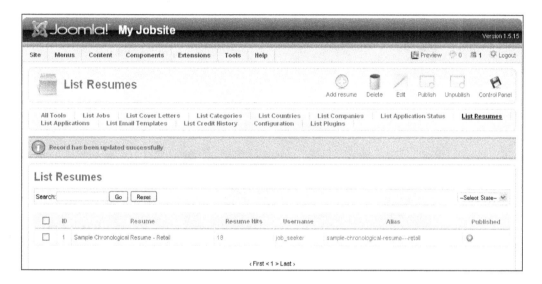

2. When the publishing status changes, you will see the message, **Record has been updated successfully**.

Deleting a resume

To delete resumes from Jobs! Pro admin panel:

1. Click on **Delete** in the **List Resumes** window.

When the publishing status changes, you will see the message, **Record has been updated successfully**.

Managing resume files

Resume files are manageable from both the Jobs! admin panel and Jobseeker panel. The Jobseeker panel will allow only managing the resume files of a specific jobseeker.

Viewing resume files

To view resume files from the Jobs! Pro admin panel:

1. Click on **List Resumes Files**.

2. The **List Resumes Files** window will open; you will see a list of resume files in this window.

Adding a new resume file

To add or upload a new resume file:

1. Click on **Add New File** in the **List Resume Files** window.

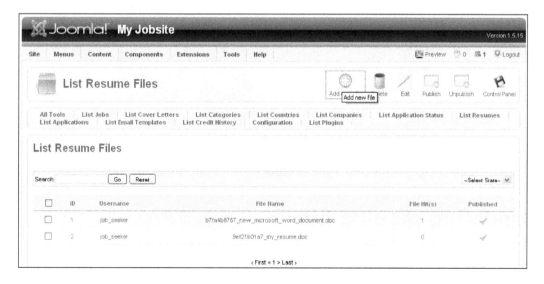

The **Add New File** window opens. In this window, you need to provide some basic information first, such as the following:

- **File Owner**: Specify the jobseeker you are uploading the resume file for. Select the username of the jobseeker in the drop-down list. You will see a letter **J** with the jobseeker's username, which helps you to identify a jobseeker.

- **File Notes**: You can write a short note for the new resume file within the 255 character limit. This note will not be visible to the user. It will only help you to identify the resume file.

- **Published**: Select the publishing status, whether it is published or unpublished.

- After providing all the information, click on **Browse** and select the resume file you want to upload. Only `.zip`, `.rar`, x-zip, `.pdf`, `.txt`, MS Word documents, `.jpeg`, `.jpg`, `.png`, and `.gif` file types are allowed. The maximum you can upload is a 2 MB-size file.

- Now click on **Save** and **Save & New** to add and upload the new resume file.

Updating resume file

In order to edit any existing resume file from the Jobs! Pro admin panel:

1. Open the **List Resume Files** window and click on **Edit** in this window.

2. The window **Update Resume File** opens. Make the changes to the information or you can select another resume file by clicking on **Browse**. The existing file will be replaced by the new resume file.

3. Now click on **Update** to save the changes you made or to replace the old resume file.

Publishing or unpublishing a resume file

To publish or unpublish any resume from Jobs! admin panel, open the **List Resume Files** window and select the resume file and then click on **Publish** or **Unpublish** in this window.

Deleting a resume file

To delete a resume file from the admin panel, click on the **Delete** icon.

Summary

In this chapter, we have learned how to view, add, delete, publish, and unpublish cover letters, resumes, and resume files. After finishing this chapter, we should be able to manage all the cover letters, resumes, and resume files. With this chapter, we have finished the Joomla! jobsite development. In the next chapter, we will learn about search engine optimization.

10
Search Engine Optimization

We can make a jobsite search engine-friendly by using some **Search Engine Optimization (SEO)** techniques to achieve a prominent ranking in most of the top search engines, such as Google, Yahoo!, Bing, and others. Before we start using search engine optimization techniques, we need to make an SEO strategy and do some research as well.

In this chapter, we'll learn:

- What is SEO
- Making SEO strategy
- Researching and choosing the right keywords
- Inserting the title and metadata in your Joomla! jobsite
- Changing basic SEO settings in Global Configuration and making search engine-friendly URLs
- Installing and using the Joomlatwork! SEO patch
- Creating an XML or HTML site map
- Submitting an XML site map using Google Webmaster Tools

Introduction

Making a Joomla! website search engine-friendly is not as difficult as people say. You can easily make your Joomla! jobsite friendlier for the search engines because Joomla! has some basic SEO settings in Global Configuration. Joomla! 1.5 has another advantage; you can enable the search engine-friendly URL option to make your website URL-friendly for any search engine. Search engine-friendly websites can improve the visibility of the website and can increase the traffic via the natural or unpaid search results. Before starting SEO, you must have some basic knowledge of the subject and need to spend a significant amount of time and effort to acquire it.

What is SEO?

SEO is an acronym for Search Engine Optimization. It is the most technical part of web marketing, which makes a website available in the top position of the search engine results to increase the website traffic. It is not advertising and it can take a few seconds or can be a regular activity. The idea behind this technique is to get a top position for a particular search term that is relevant to your site and not because you have paid for it. There are many ways to achieve a better ranking in the search engine results, but if you want to get a better result, you need to update your site frequently with search engine-friendly content.

Making an SEO strategy

To improve a website ranking in the search engine, you need to do some research first and also you need to make an SEO strategy for your website. This strategy will guide you to make your website **Search Engine-Friendly (SEF)**. Create a list of stepwise tasks you want to finish. You can apply the following SEO strategy for your Joomla! jobsite:

1. Research and choose the right keywords.
2. Insert the title and metadata in your Joomla! jobsite.
3. Change basic SEO settings in Global Configuration.
4. Installing and using Joomlatwork! SEO patch.
5. Create an XML or HTML site map.
6. Submit your website to search engines.
7. Submit an XML site map using Google webmaster tools.

Researching and choosing the right keywords

Keyword means the word or phrase that people enter into a search engine to find what they are looking for. Do some research for good keywords that are relevant to your jobsite and then choose the right keywords for your site. Getting the right keywords is very important for driving traffic to your site. This is also an important part of search engine marketing. Choosing the right keyword is essential, and you should give it first priority. Before choosing a keyword, you should consider the following things:

- Try to understand what people may type in the search box while looking for a site. Don't try to optimize a single page for every keyword.

- You shouldn't use general keywords, such as jobs, finance, technology, and other such words. You can use a general keyword with a specific word, for example, *finance jobs in UK*.

- Search for your competitors' sites and review what keywords they're using. But do not copy anything.

- Spend as much time as possible to research your keywords.

You can use search engines, such as Yahoo!, Google, Bing, ASK, and others to check your keywords. Enter your keyword in the search box and wait for a few seconds. You will see some keyword suggestions. Analyze them and choose the appropriate one as your keyword. For the best output, choose the word that is searched often but has less competition.

You shouldn't use search engine stop words in your keyword because most search engines omit and filter out common words to save disk spaces or to speed up search results. These filtered words are known as **stop words**.

 However, not all search engines use the same stop words. See *Appendix B* to view a list of words that are filtered by most search engines.

Also, there are some tools available on the Internet that help to find the right keywords. For example, **Word Tracker** is the most popular keyword research tool. You can get it from the website `www.wordtracker.com`.

Inserting the title and metadata in your Joomla! jobsite

Inserting a corresponding title and metadata is very important to get a page in a search engine. You can insert title and metadata in Joomla! **Global Configuration**:

1. Select the menu **Site | Global configuration** from Joomla! admin panel and go to **Global configuration** window. Now enter your title in the **Site Name** field of the **Site Settings** area. This title must be relevant to your site. The title will be shown at the top of the browser and will be used as a heading in the search results.

2. Enter a short description containing the most important keywords of your jobsite in **Global Site Meta Description** field, and also type your keywords separating each with a comma in the **Global Site Meta Keywords** field of **Metadata Settings** section.

Site Settings	
Site Offline	⊙ No ○ Yes
Offline Message	This site is currently offline!
Site Name	nancial Jobs Services - Entry level inance Jobs
Default WYSIWYG Editor	Editor - TinyMCE ▾
List Length	20 ▾
Feed length	10 ▾
Feed Email	Author E-mail ▾

Metadata Settings	
Global Site Meta Description	Financial Jobs Services - Financial Jobs Services provided by Financial Jobs Services Ltd
Global Site Meta Keywords	Financial Jobsite, Financial Jobs, Financial Jobs Services, Jobs Services, Financial career
Show Title Meta Tag	○ No ⊙ Yes
Show Author Meta Tag	○ No ⊙ Yes

Changing basic SEO settings in Global Configuration

The Joomla! 1.5 contains some basic SEO settings in Global Configuration. You need to change some default SEO settings to enable more functionality. By default, the Joomla! Search Engine-Friendly(SEF) functionality is not enabled; this means that the URLs of your site will look like the following:

```
http://www.yourdomain.com/index.php?option=com_content&view=article&id=1&Itemid=2.
```

This URL is complex and not search engine-friendly. If we change the link to something like the following:

```
http://www.yourdomain.com/contact
```

it will be a meaningful and search engine-friendly URL. To enable search engine-friendly URL functionality for your site, follow these steps:

1. You can enable the `mod_rewrite` function. You must confirm first that the `mod_rewrite` is installed on your server. `mod_rewrite` is an Apache web server module. `mod_rewrite` provides a powerful way to do URL manipulations and removes the dynamic portion of the URL, effectively making it static, thus preventing potential conflicts and increasing site visibility.

2. In order to enable the rewrite rules, you have to rename the `htaccess.txt` file in your Joomla! installation directory to `.htaccess`. The `.htaccess` is a configuration file for use on web servers running the Apache Web Server software.

3. Now log into the Joomla! 1.5 admin panel and then go to the **Global Configuration** window by clicking on the menu **Site | Global configuration** to change the Joomla! SEO settings.

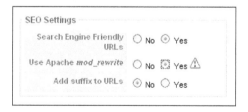

4. In the **SEO Settings** section, change **Search Engine Friendly URLs** and **Use Apache mod_rewrite** options value to **Yes**. You can add a suffix (`.html`) to the URLs. After this, click on **Save** in the top right-hand side of this window.

Installing and using Joomlatwork! SEO patch

Joomlatwork! SEO patch is a non-commercial patch package. You can improve the SEO settings of Joomla! with this free SEO patch package for Joomla!1.5 stable and higher. This patch solves the issues regarding the settings within the HTML head section of your HTML page. The patch will allow us to control title and metadata settings in the `http` header settings of Joomla! site pages. You can get this product absolutely free from its official website link:

`http://www.joomlatwork.com/products/free-downloads/seo-patch-joomla-15.html`.

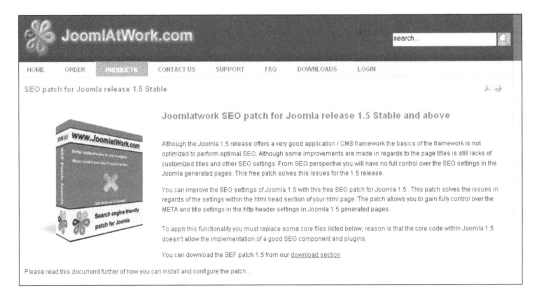

Download the patch file that matches your Joomla! version, and after the download, extract the `*.zip` file within the directory. After this, upload the files to the directory where you have installed Joomla! site (you can use FTP to upload your files to the server). The patch files will replace Joomla! standard files.

 If you have a problem with this patch, you can download the redo patch file that contains the Joomla! standard files and will bring your Joomla! installation back into the default Joomla! settings.

After installing this patch, log in to the Joomla! 1.5 admin panel. Go to the **Global configuration** window by selecting the menu **Site | Global configuration**.

Now click on the **SEO** tab. In this window, we need to define two settings—**Metafields Settings** and **Metadata Settings**.

We have to provide information in the **Metafields Settings** area, as shown:

- **HTML Title setting**: You may see this field empty if the setting is not saved within the global configuration file. To display the title on your pages, you can at least put the **[TITLE]** tag in this field.

- **Default title**: The value of this field will be displayed if there is no title available for a specific page. You can insert the **[SITENAME]** tag in the field.

- **Meta tag robots settings**: In the standard setting of Joomla!, the robot tag value is always `index` and `follow` and you cannot change this value. But this option enables you to change the default value of a robot tag. If you do not want to display any robot tag, select the value **Don't display robot tag**.

- **Show title Meta tag**: You can select the value whether **Yes** or **No**. Select the value **Yes** to set a Meta tag title in the HTML head section with the value of the title.

- **Show Author Meta tag**: Select the value **Yes** to set a Meta tag called author within the HTML head section.

- **Show joomla generator tag**: This function will remove the default generator tag that is generated by Joomla!. You can also set your own value to the **Generator tag** field in the **Metadata Settings**.

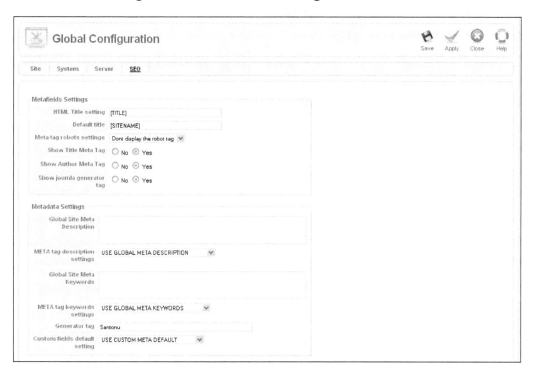

After providing this information, you can change the default Meta tags settings. By using Meta tag description settings and the Meta tag keywords settings, you can set default value when no description or keywords are declared to content or a menu item. You can also add custom Meta fields through `metaconfig.xml` file in your server root directory.

Creating an XML or HTML site map

A site map is a file created by XML, HTML, or other language that lists all the URLs of a website and helps search engines (such as Yahoo!, Google) to crawl the website accordingly. You need to submit an XML or HTML site map in different search engines to make all the pages of your website available. You can easily create your site map without having any knowledge of the markup languages. There are a lot of software, applications, and websites available that enable you to create a site map automatically in various file types. One of the most popular websites for generating a site map is `http://www.xml-sitemaps.com/`. It provides an online tool that will help you to create your site map in a few seconds.

You need to provide some information to generate the new site map, as shown:

1. **Starting URL**: Please enter the full URL (including the `'http://'` prefix) of your site in this field. For example:

    `http://www.myjobsite.net/.`

2. **Change frequency**: This value indicates how frequently the content of a particular URL may change. Select any values from the list, such as **None**, **Always**, **Hourly**, **Daily**. If you select the value **Daily**, it means that your website content is changed every day.

3. **Last Modified**: It displays the date and time the URL was last modified. This information allows the crawlers to avoid crawling a document again, if the document has not been modified. Here you can specify your own date and time or can enable the usage of your server's response headers.

4. **Priority**: You can select the value **Automatic Priority** from the list to assign priority automatically. The priority of a particular URL is relative to the other pages on the same website.

5. After providing this information, click on **Start**. The progress will be indicated; wait until the website is successfully crawled.

6. You will see the generated site map details page, including the number of pages, list of the broken links, XML site map content, and links to the compressed site map.

7. Download the site map file using this link or copy from the XML site map content area and save it with an extension .xml in a text editor. Upload it into your server root directory where we have installed Joomla!.

Submitting your website to a search engine

Submitting a new website to the search engines is an important task in order to make it available on search engines. You can submit your jobsite address to the top search engines, such as Google, Yahoo!, and others. There are lots of tools and software available to automatically submit websites to search engines. But it is better to submit your website manually.

1. To submit your site to Google, open the website link, `http://www.google.com/addurl/`, in your web browser.

2. Enter your URL in the **URL** field. Please enter your full URL, including the '`http://`' prefix. For example: `http://www.myjobsite.com/`. You can also insert a comment.

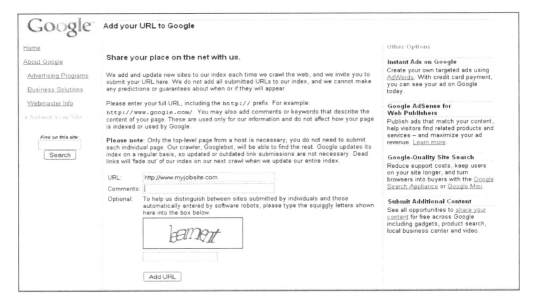

3. You also need to provide a Captcha verification code. Click on **Add URL** to submit your website URL. Your website will be submitted to Google and you will see a confirmation with a 'thank you' message.

4. If you want to submit your site on Yahoo!, you can submit your website easily. Go to the website link: `http://siteexplorer.search.yahoo.com/submit`. You must sign in with a Yahoo! ID or sign up for free in order to do this. After signing in, enter the URL of the website you'd like to submit to be included in the Yahoo! search index, and click on **Submit URL**.

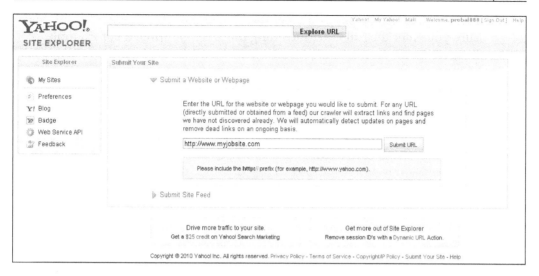

5. Your website will be submitted to Yahoo! and you will see a thank you message. It may take a few weeks for your website to be included in the search index.

Submitting XML site map using Google webmaster tools

Google webmaster tools enable you to submit your site map and help crawling and indexing your website. To use Google webmaster tools:

1. Go to the website link `http://www.google.com/webmasters`.

2. Sign in or sign up for a new account. After signing in, you will be redirected to Google webmaster tools home page.

3. Now click on **Add a site** and enter the URL of the site you want to add. Make sure you enter the full URL, including the 'http://' prefix. For example http://www.myjobsite.com/.

4. Click on **Continue**. The **Verify ownership** page opens. Select a verification method you want, and follow the instructions. It will verify that you are the owner of this website.

5. Once the site is verified, click on the website link and it opens **Dashboard** window. Look at the bottom right of this window; you will see **Submit a Sitemap** link. Now click on this link, the window **Sitemaps** opens.

6. Now click on **Submit a Sitemap**. Define where your website is located and click on **Submit Sitemap** – your site map will be submitted to Google. You will see your site map status and total submitted URLs in the table.

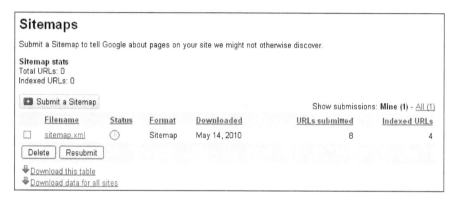

Summary

This chapter provided guidelines for basic search engine optimization techniques. In this chapter, we learned SEO, making SEO strategy, how to choose the right keywords, inserting the title and metadata in your Joomla! jobsite, changing the basic SEO settings, making SEF URLs, creating an XML or HTML site map, submitting a site map and website to search engines.

A
Online Resource

For more information regarding the contents of this book, you may find the following online resources useful:

- Joomla! 1.5 Download:

  `http://www.joomla.org/download.html`

- Joomla! 1.5 Demo:

  `http://demo.joomla.org/`

- Joomla! Extension Directory:

  `http://extensions.joomla.org/`

- Joomla! Official Documentation:

  `http://docs.joomla.org/`

- Joomla! Template:

  `http://www.joomlart.com`

  `http://www.123webdesign.com`

  `http://www.siteground.com/joomla-hosting/joomla-templates.htm`

  `http://www.joomla24.com/`

  `http://www.joomlashack.com/`

- Joomla! SEO:

  `http://www.pathos-seo.com/`

  `http://seo4joomla.wordpress.com/`

  `http://www.joomlaseo.net/`

  `http://www.compassdesigns.net/joomla-blog/top-10-joomla-seo-tips-for-google`

- IknJobs! 1.3.x:

  `http://www.instantphp.com/store/details/6/jobs.html`

- XHTML:

  `http://www.w3.org/TR/xhtml1/`

  `http://en.wikipedia.org/wiki/XHTML`

  `http://www.w3schools.com/xhtml/`

  `http://www.freewebmasterhelp.com/tutorials/xhtml`

  `http://xhtml.com/en/xhtml/reference/`

- CSS:

  `http://www.w3.org/Style/CSS/`

  `http://en.wikipedia.org/wiki/Cascading_Style_Sheets`

  `http://www.w3schools.com/css/`

  `http://www.echoecho.com/cssintroduction.htm`

  `http://www.html.net/tutorials/css/`

- XML:

  `http://www.w3.org/XML/`

  `http://en.wikipedia.org/wiki/XML`

  `http://www.w3schools.com/xml/default.asp`

- PHP & MySQL:

  `http://www.php.net`

  `http://www.mysql.com/`

  `http://en.wikipedia.org/wiki/PHP`

  `http://www.w3schools.com/PHP/`

  `http://www.w3schools.com/php/php_mysql_intro.asp`

  `http://www.freewebmasterhelp.com/tutorials/phpmysql`

- XAMPP:

  `http://www.apachefriends.org/en/xampp.html`

  `http://sourceforge.net/projects/xampp/`

  `http://en.wikipedia.org/wiki/XAMPP`

  `http://keito.me/tutorials/xampp`

- phpMyAdmin:

  `http://www.phpmyadmin.net/home_page/index.php`

B
Search Engine Stop Words

Stop words are filtered by search engines. The following table shows a list of the words that are omitted by most of the search engines. Do not use these in your jobsite's **Title**, **Meta Description**, and **Meta Keyword** fields.

a	f	meanwhile	su
about	few	mg	such
above	fi	mh	sv
according	fifty	microsoft	sy
across	find	might	sz
actually	first	mil	t
ad	five	million	taking
adj	fj	miss	tc
ae	fk	mk	td
af	fm	ml	ten
after	fo	mm	text
afterwards	for	mn	tf
ag	former	mo	tg
again	formerly	more	test
against	forty	moreover	th
ai	found	most	than
al	four	mostly	that

all	fr	mp	that'll
almost	free	mq	that's
alone	from	mr	the
along	further	mrs	their
already	fx	ms	them
also	g	msie	themselves
although	ga	mt	then
always	gb	mu	thence
am	gd	much	there
among	ge	must	there'll
amongst	get	mv	there's
an	gf	mw	thousand
and	gg	mx	three
another	gh	my	through
any	gi	myself	throughout
anyhow	gl	mz	thru
anyone	gm	n	thus
anything	gmt	na	tj
anywhere	gn	namely	tk
ao	go	nc	tm
aq	gov	ne	tn
ar	gp	neither	to
are	gq	net	together
aren	gr	netscape	too
aren't	gs	never	toward
around	gt	nevertheless	towards
arpa	gu	new	tp

as	gw	next	tr
at	gy	nf	trillion
au	h	ng	tt
aw	had	ni	tv
az	has	nine	tw
b	hasn	ninety	twenty
ba	hasn't	nl	two
bb	have	no	tz
bd	haven	nobody	u
be	haven't	o	ua
became	he	of	ug
because	he'd	off	uk
become	he'll	often	um
becomes	he's	om	under
becoming	help	on	unless
been	hence	once	unlike
before	her	one	unlikely
beforehand	here	one's	until
begin	here's	only	up
beginning	hereafter	onto	upon
behind	hereby	or	us
being	herein	org	use
below	hereupon	other	used
beside	hers	others	using
besides	herself	otherwise	uy
between	him	our	uz
beyond	himself	ours	v

bf	his	ourselves	va
bg	hk	out	vc
bh	hm	over	ve
bi	hn	overall	very
billion	home	own	vg
bj	homepage	p	vi
bm	how	pa	via
bn	however	page	vn
bo	hr	pe	vu
both	ht	per	w
br	htm	perhaps	was
bs	html	pf	wasn
bt	http	pg	wasn't
but	hu	ph	we
buy	hundred	pk	we'd
bv	i	pl	we'll
bw	i'd	pm	we're
by	i'll	pn	we've
bz	i'm	pr	web
c	i've	pt	webpage
ca	i.e.	pw	website
can	id	py	welcome
can't	ie	q	well
cannot	if	qa	were
caption	il	r	weren
cc	im	rather	weren't
cd	in	re	wf

cf	inc	recent	what
cg	j	recently	what'll
ch	je	reserved	what's
ci	jm	ring	whatever
ck	jo	ro	when
cl	join	ru	whence
click	jp	rw	whenever
cm	k	s	where
cn	ke	sa	whereafter
co	kg	same	whereas
co.	kh	sb	whereby
com	ki	sc	wherein
copy	km	sd	whereupon
could	kn	se	wherever
couldn	kp	seem	whether
couldn't	kr	seemed	which
cr	kw	seeming	while
cs	ky	seems	whither
cu	kz	seven	who
cv	l	seventy	who'd
cx	la	several	who'll
cy	last	sg	who's
cz	later	sh	whoever
d	latter	she	NULL
de	lb	she'd	whole
did	lc	she'll	whom
e	least	she's	whomever
each	less	should	whose

ec	let	shouldn	why
edu	let's	shouldn't	will
ee	li	si	with
eg	like	since	within
eh	likely	site	without
eight	lk	six	won
eighty	ll	sixty	won't
either	ls	sj	would
else	lt	sk	wouldn
elsewhere	ltd	sl	wouldn't
end	lu	sm	ws
ending	lv	sn	www
enough	ly	so	x
er	m	some	y
es	ma	somehow	ye
et	made	someone	yes
etc	make	something	yet
even	makes	sometime	you
ever	many	sometimes	you'd
every	maybe	somewhere	you'll
everyone	mc	sr	you're
everything	md	st	you've
everywhere	me	still	your
except	meantime	stop	yours
			yourself
			yourselves
			yt

Index

Thank you for buying
Building job sites with Joomla!

About Packt Publishing

Packt, pronounced 'packed', published its first book "*Mastering phpMyAdmin for Effective MySQL Management*" in April 2004 and subsequently continued to specialize in publishing highly focused books on specific technologies and solutions.

Our books and publications share the experiences of your fellow IT professionals in adapting and customizing today's systems, applications, and frameworks. Our solution based books give you the knowledge and power to customize the software and technologies you're using to get the job done. Packt books are more specific and less general than the IT books you have seen in the past. Our unique business model allows us to bring you more focused information, giving you more of what you need to know, and less of what you don't.

Packt is a modern, yet unique publishing company, which focuses on producing quality, cutting-edge books for communities of developers, administrators, and newbies alike. For more information, please visit our website: www.packtpub.com.

About Packt Open Source

In 2010, Packt launched two new brands, Packt Open Source and Packt Enterprise, in order to continue its focus on specialization. This book is part of the Packt Open Source brand, home to books published on software built around Open Source licences, and offering information to anybody from advanced developers to budding web designers. The Open Source brand also runs Packt's Open Source Royalty Scheme, by which Packt gives a royalty to each Open Source project about whose software a book is sold.

Writing for Packt

We welcome all inquiries from people who are interested in authoring. Book proposals should be sent to author@packtpub.com. If your book idea is still at an early stage and you would like to discuss it first before writing a formal book proposal, contact us; one of our commissioning editors will get in touch with you.

We're not just looking for published authors; if you have strong technical skills but no writing experience, our experienced editors can help you develop a writing career, or simply get some additional reward for your expertise.

Learning Joomla! 1.5 Extension Development: Creating Modules, Components, and Plugins with PHP

ISBN: 978-1-847191-30-4   Paperback: 176 pages

A practical tutorial for creating your first Joomla! 1.5 extensions with PHP

1. Program your own extensions to Joomla!

2. Create new, self-contained components with both back-end and front-end functionality

3. Create configurable site modules to show information on every page

Joomla! 1.5 SEO

ISBN: 978-1-847198-16-7   Paperback: 324 pages

Improve the search engine friendliness of your web site

1. Improve the rankings of your Joomla! site in the search engine result pages such as Google, Yahoo, and Bing

2. Improve your web site SEO performance by gaining and producing incoming links to your web site

3. Market and measure the success of your blog by applying SEO

4. Integrate analytics and paid advertising into your Joomla! blog

Please check **www.PacktPub.com** for information on our titles

www.ingramcontent.com/pod-product-compliance
Lightning Source LLC
Chambersburg PA
CBHW060547060326
40690CB00017B/3636